GOING INTO TOWN

BY THE SAME AUTHOR

Can't We Talk About Something More Pleasant?

What I Hate from A to Z

Theories of Everything

The Party, After You Left

Childproof

Mondo Boxo

Proof of Life on Earth

The Four Elements

Parallel Universes

Unscientific Americans

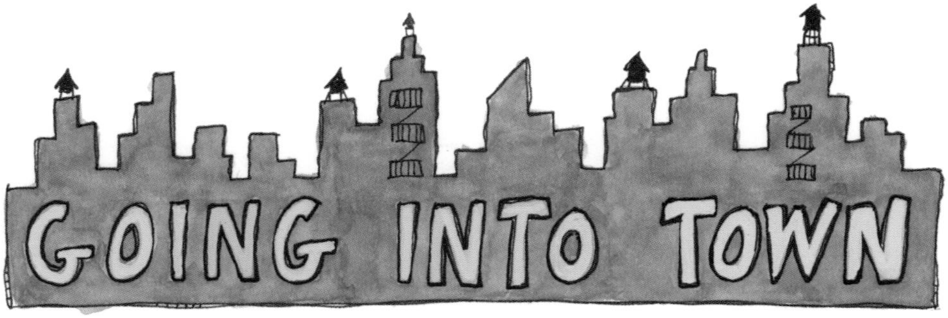
GOING INTO TOWN

A Love Letter to New York

Roz Chast

BLOOMSBURY
New York London Oxford New Delhi Sydney

Bloomsbury USA

An imprint of Bloomsbury Publishing Plc

1385 Broadway
New York
NY 10018
USA

50 Bedford Square
London
WC1B 3DP
UK

www.bloomsbury.com

BLOOMSBURY and the Diana logo are trademarks of Bloomsbury Publishing Plc

First published 2017

ISBN: HB: 978-1-62040-321-1
ePub: 978-1-63286-978-4

LIBRARY OF CONGRESS CATALOGING-IN-PUBLICATION DATA IS AVAILABLE.

2 4 6 8 10 9 7 5 3 1

Printed and bound in China at C&C Offset Printing Co. Ltd

To find out more about our authors and books visit www.bloomsbury.com. Here you will find extracts, author interviews, details of forthcoming events, and the option to sign up for our newsletters.

Bloomsbury books may be purchased for business or promotional use. For information on bulk purchases please contact Macmillan Corporate and Premium Sales Department at specialmarkets@macmillan.com.

CONTENTS:

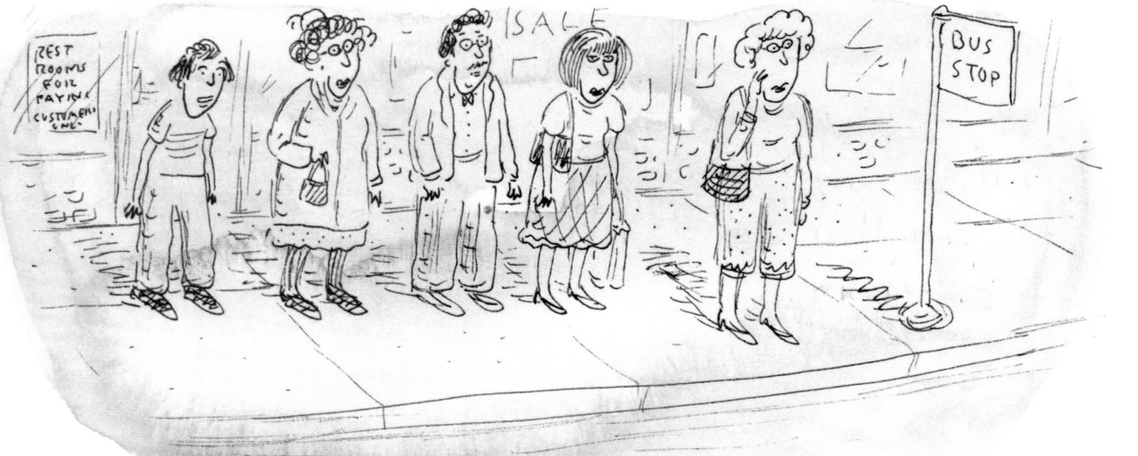

REST ROOMS FOR PAYING CUSTOMERS ONLY
BUS STOP

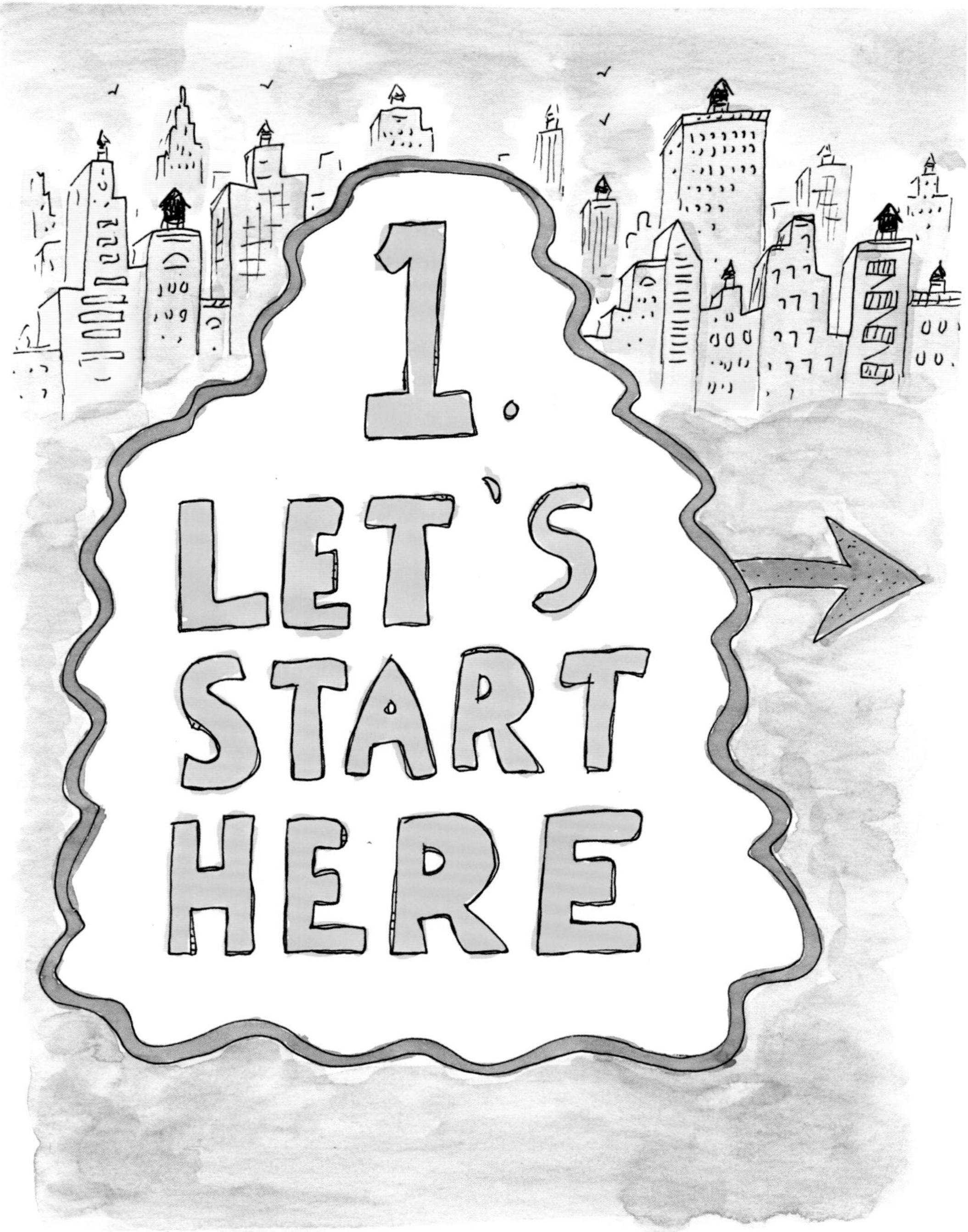
1.
LET'S
START
HERE

This is not a "definitive guide book" to Manhattan. In fact, it's not really a guide book. There's nothing in here about the Statue of Liberty, for example. Why? Because I've never been. I'd *like* to go. Someday. Just not today. Please don't make me go today.

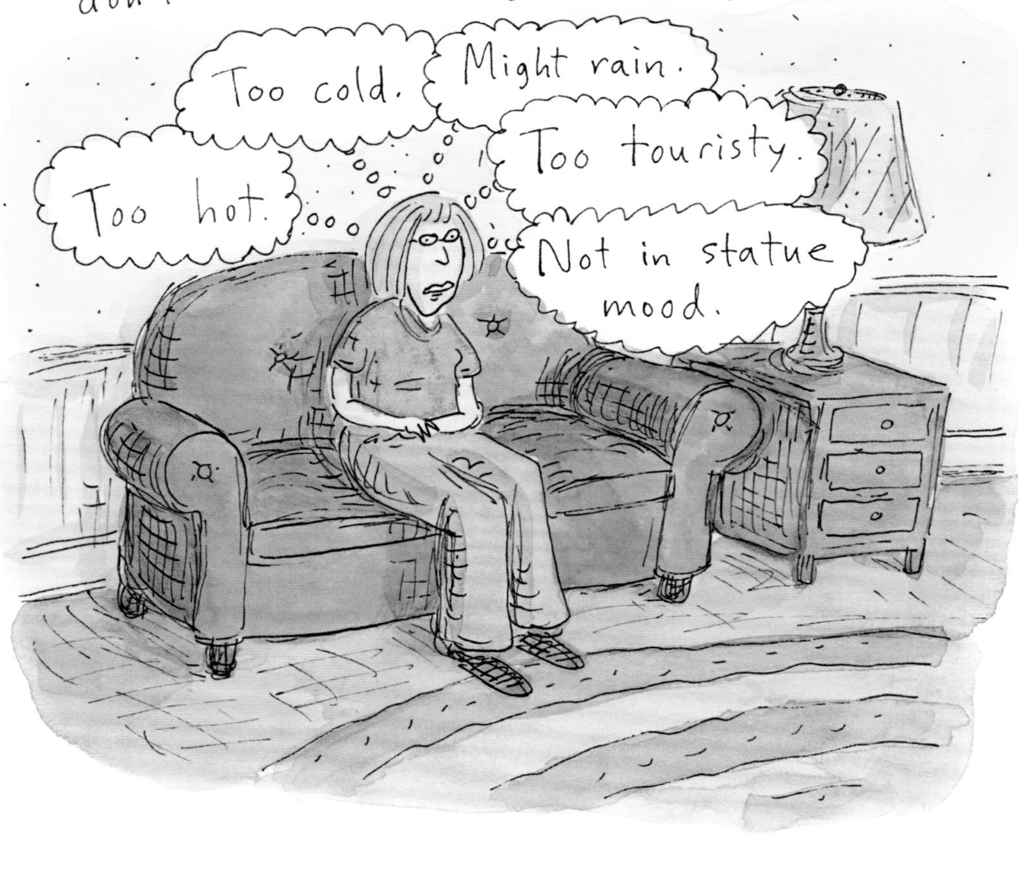
Too hot.
Too cold.
Might rain.
Too touristy.
Not in statue mood.

This is also definitely not one of those "insider's guides" where I tell you about the hippest clubs, the swankiest restaurants, the edgiest neighborhoods, the coolest gyms, or the store where the best people buy the most exclusive shoes.

It's not a history book. Do not imagine, even for a second, that I'm going to tell you a bunch of cool facts, like how Betsy Ross invented concrete, or that a thousand feet under Grand Central, somebody discovered an old Pilgrim restaurant, and look, here's the menu:

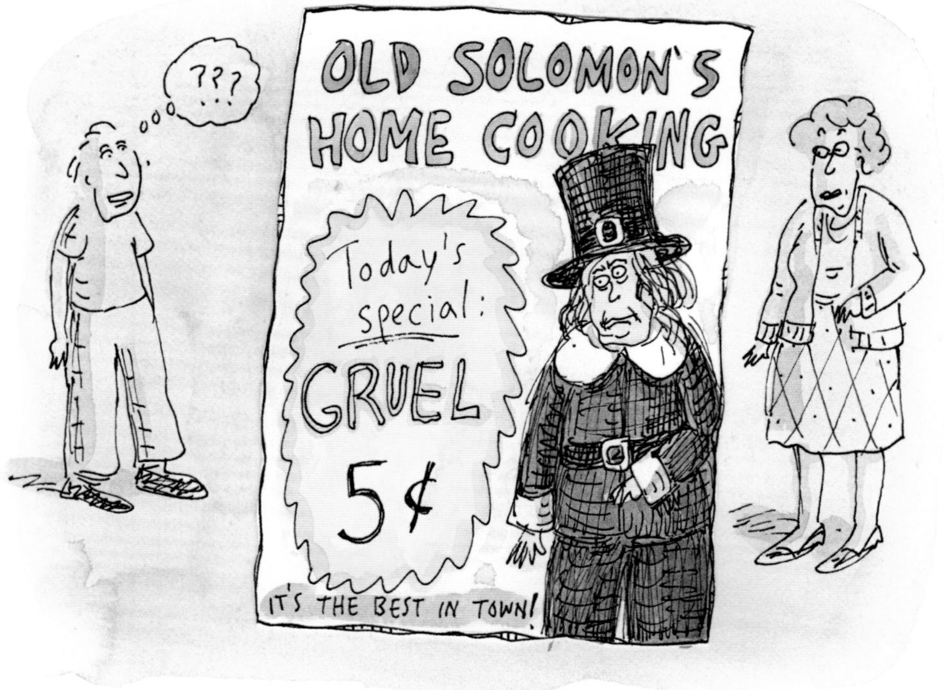
???
OLD SOLOMON'S HOME COOKING
Today's special:
GRUEL
5¢
IT'S THE BEST IN TOWN!

It began as a small booklet
I made for my daughter before
she left her home in Suburbia to
attend college in Manhattan:

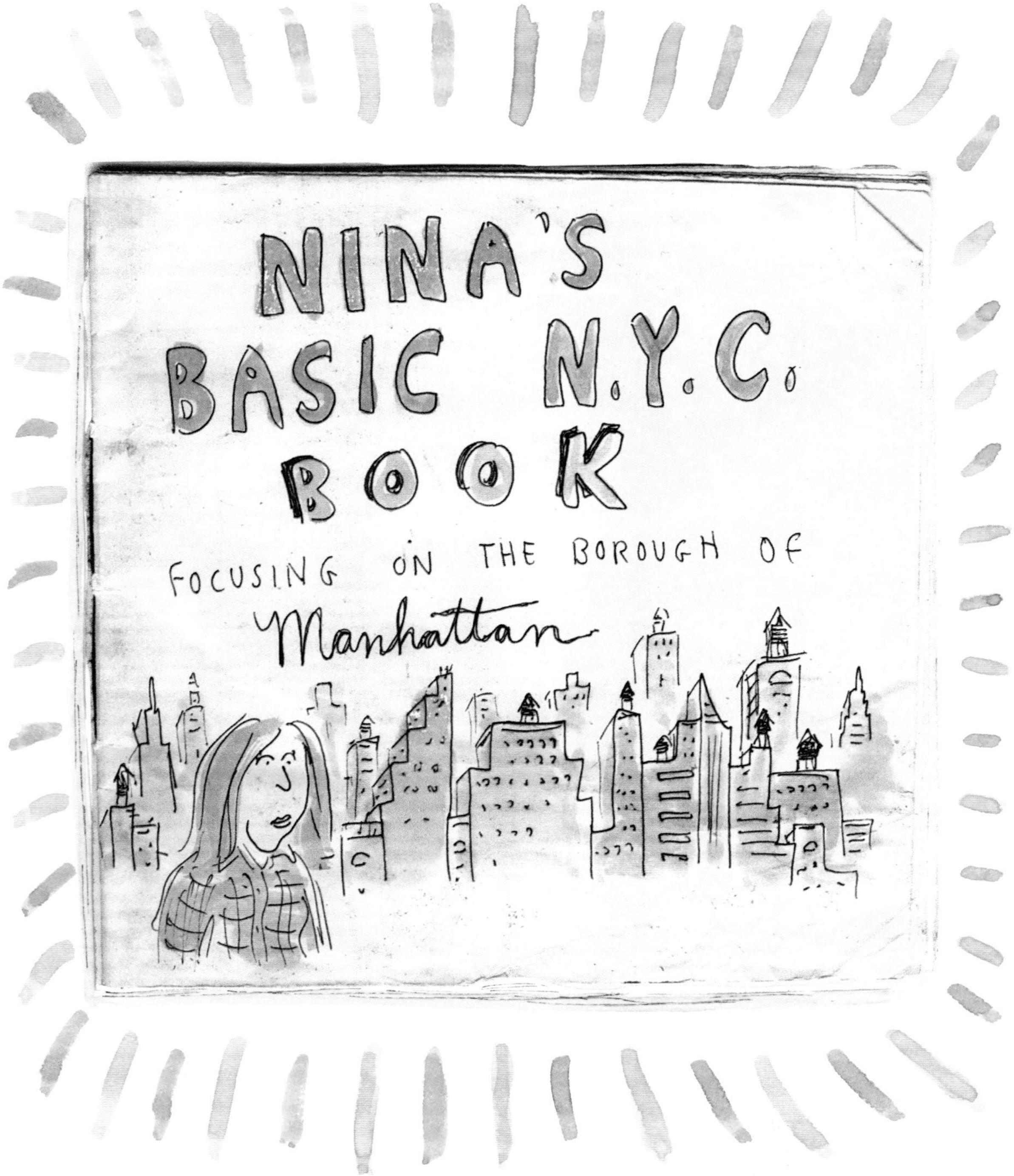
NINA'S
BASIC N.Y.C.
BOOK
FOCUSING ON THE BOROUGH OF
Manhattan

BUT FIRST, A LITTLE BACKGROUND:

When our son was almost three and I was pregnant with our second child, my husband, our son, and I left Brooklyn for a pretty, leafy suburb about an hour north of Manhattan.

There were five main reasons for this leap into The Unknown:

① This was 1990 — the middle of the crack epidemic. We'd had it with crime, the crack vials all over the sidewalk — all of it.

Mommy, what dat?

I eat dat.

(2) free, excellent public schools where we were going.

(3) My parents lived in Brooklyn for some people, this would have been a plus, but I had "mixed feelings."

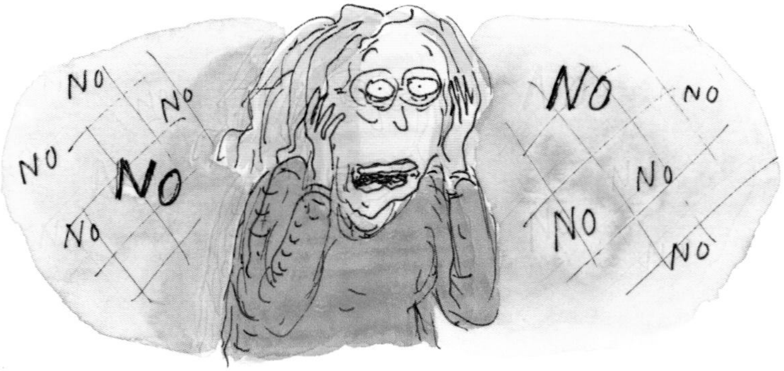
NO
NO
NO
NO
NO
NO
NO
NO
NO
NO

(4) Sometimes, when you grow up in a place, you need to get away. I saw Brooklyn differently from people who came there from Wisconsin or wherever. Behind every cute organic food store, I saw the ghost of the sad, dark, odiferous grocerette of my childhood. There was nothing there for me.

(5) But the main reason was this: we couldn't afford the space we needed. The four-bedroom house we bought in Suburbia cost less than a crappy two-bedroom walk-up in Brooklyn, even in 1990.

The decision to leave the city was

TERRIFYING.

Must... play... soccer...
Need... mall... now...
Lawn... extremely... important...
Hell... with... art... Collect... thimbles... instead...

I didn't know how to drive. I didn't like the idea of living directly on top of a boiler or a furnace or whatever the hell was in a house basement. I'd never lived in what my parents called "the country." Also, would we turn into philistines? ZOMBIES???

...REPUBLICANS???

But in 1990...

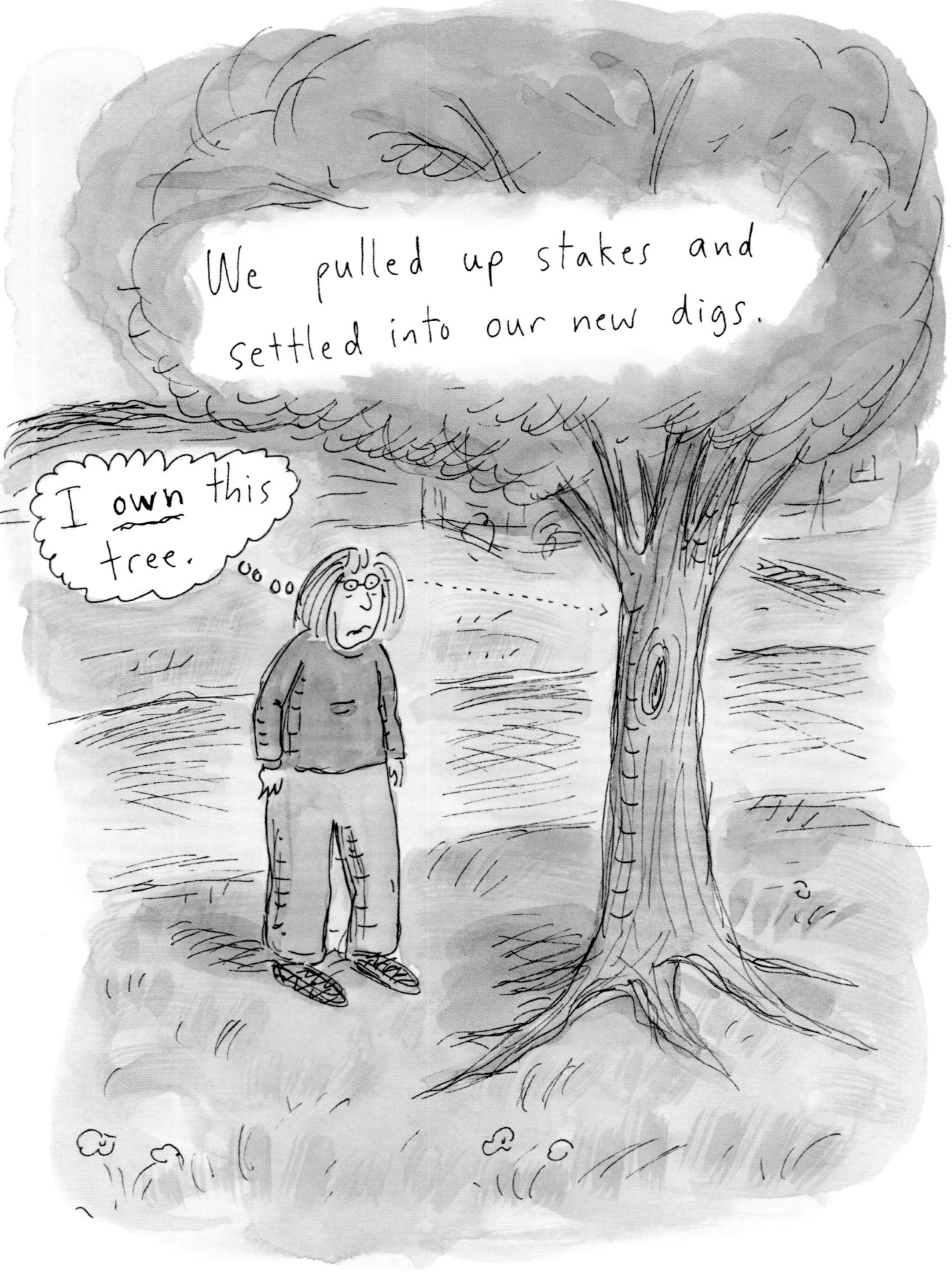
We pulled up stakes and settled into our new digs.
I own this tree.

As our kids were growing up, I frequently took them into the city. I wanted them to share my love for my hometown. But about a week before my daughter left for college in Manhattan, I decided to check up on her sense of "logistics."

HERE'S WHAT HAPPENED:

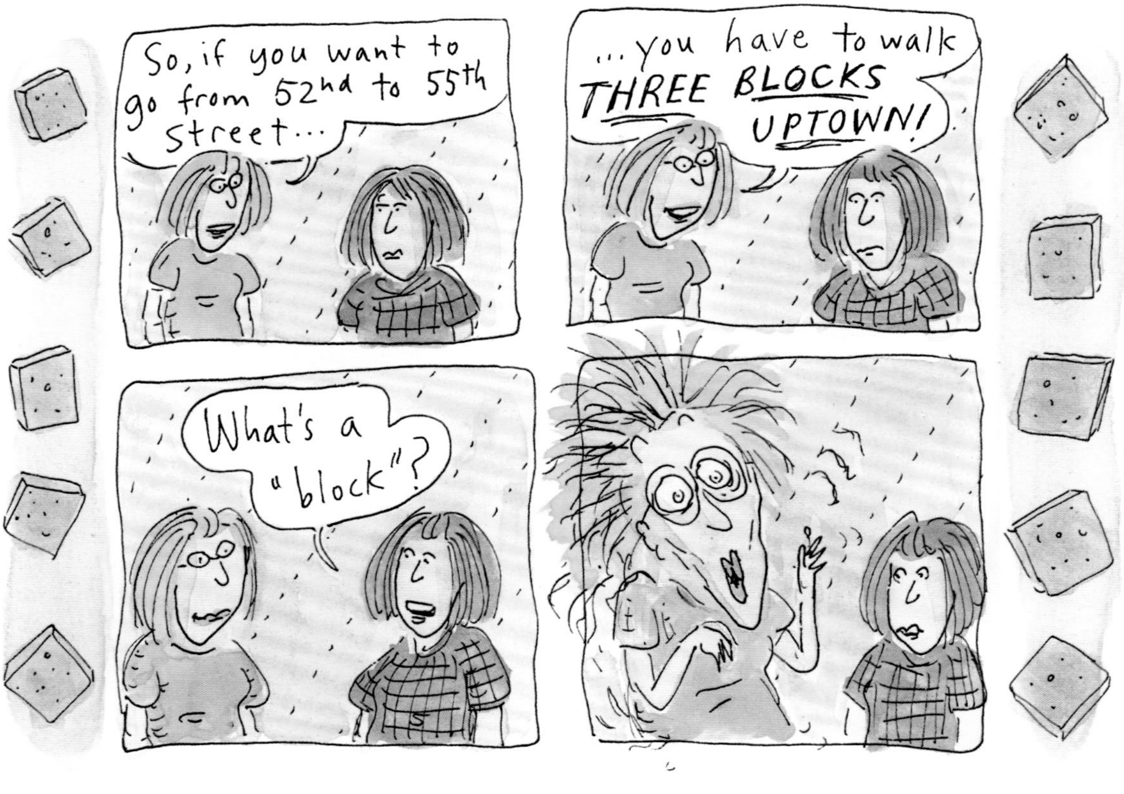
So, if you want to go from 52nd to 55th street...
...you have to walk THREE BLOCKS UPTOWN!
What's a "block"?

Maybe she was yanking my chain. But on the off chance that her childhood in Prettyville, U.S.A., had truly stunted her block-understanding, I decided to make her a little booklet containing some basic stuff about Manhattan, where she would be living, at least for the first year. Something she could carry around in her back pocket. Some maps, some tips. Nothing too overwhelming.

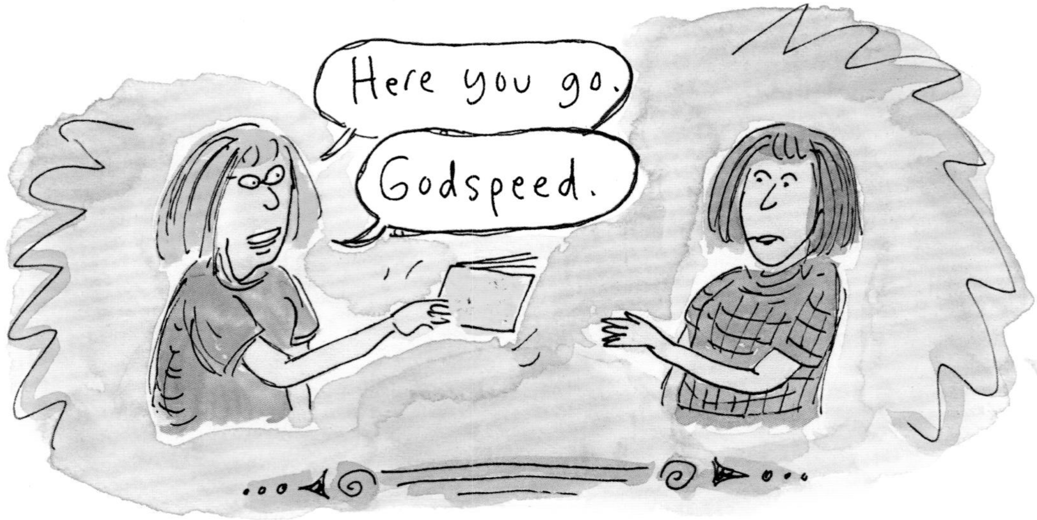
Here you go.
Godspeed.

When I gave her that book, I had this hope: that if she had the right tools for getting around the city, and of course, some luck, because one always needs luck, especially in New York, she would fall in love with the city, the way I did when I was just a few years older than her. I wanted to introduce her to Manhattan and didn't want them to "get off on the wrong foot."

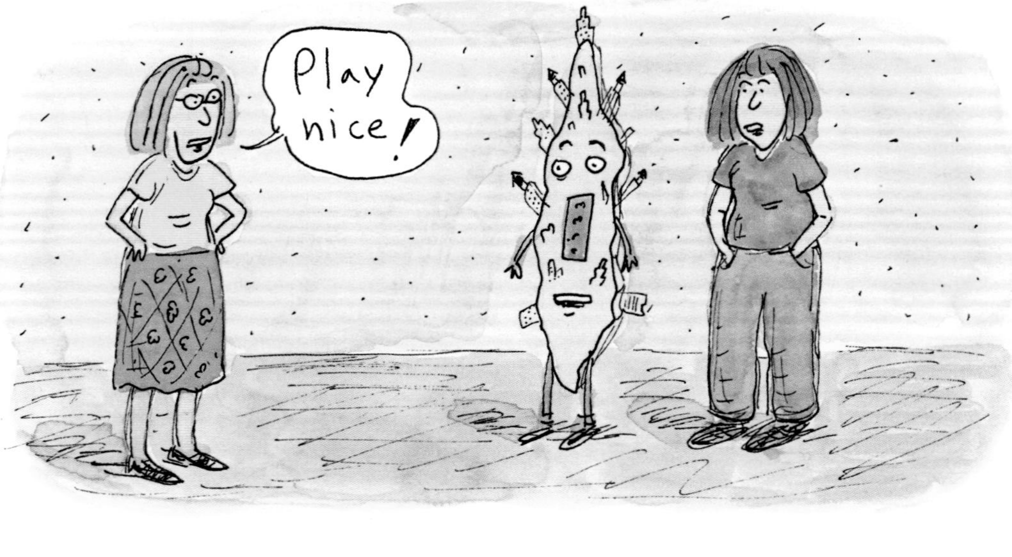
Play nice!

QUESTIONS ASKED BY

The Suburban Child

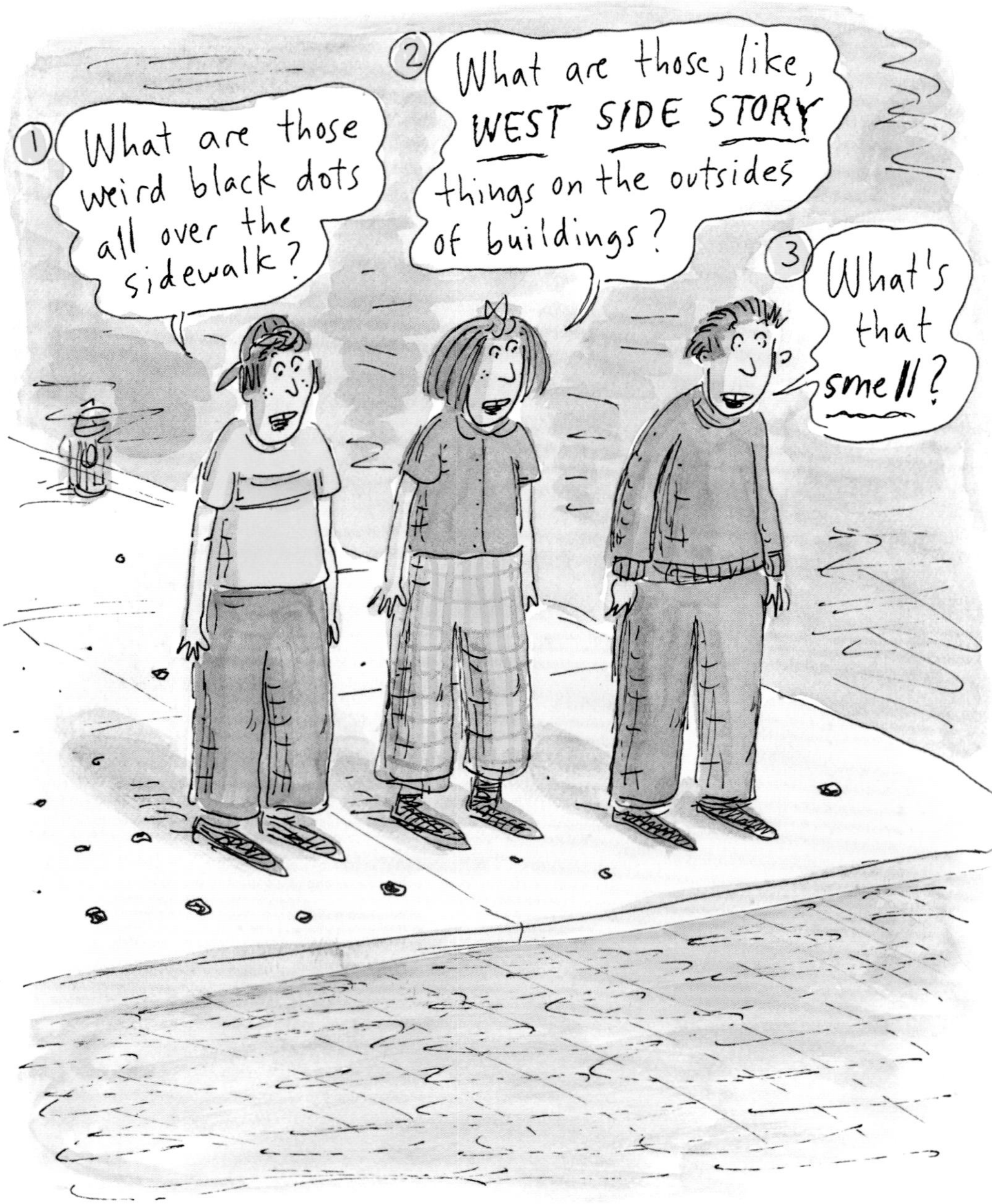
1
What are those weird black dots all over the sidewalk?
2
What are those, like, WEST SIDE STORY things on the outsides of buildings?
3
What's that smell?

ANSWERS:

① Gum (probably)

② Fire escapes

③ I don't know, but let's keep walking.

°°°○◁▭▷○°°

I feel about Manhattan the way I feel about a book, a TV series, a movie, a play, an artist, a song, a food, a _whatever_ that I love. I want to tell you about it so that maybe you will love it too. I'm not worried about it being "ruined" by too many people "discovering" it. Manhattan's been ruined since 1626, when Peter Minuit bought it from Native Americans for $ 24.$\underline{00}$.

°°°○◁▭▷○°°

Now my kids are grown-ups. The city has changed since I was 23. Things have happened. Some good, some bad, some very bad. But I still love it more than any place else, and hope you will too.

I'm walkin' heah.

2

BASIC LAYOUT

OF MANHATTAN

(I'm not kidding. You really need to know this.)

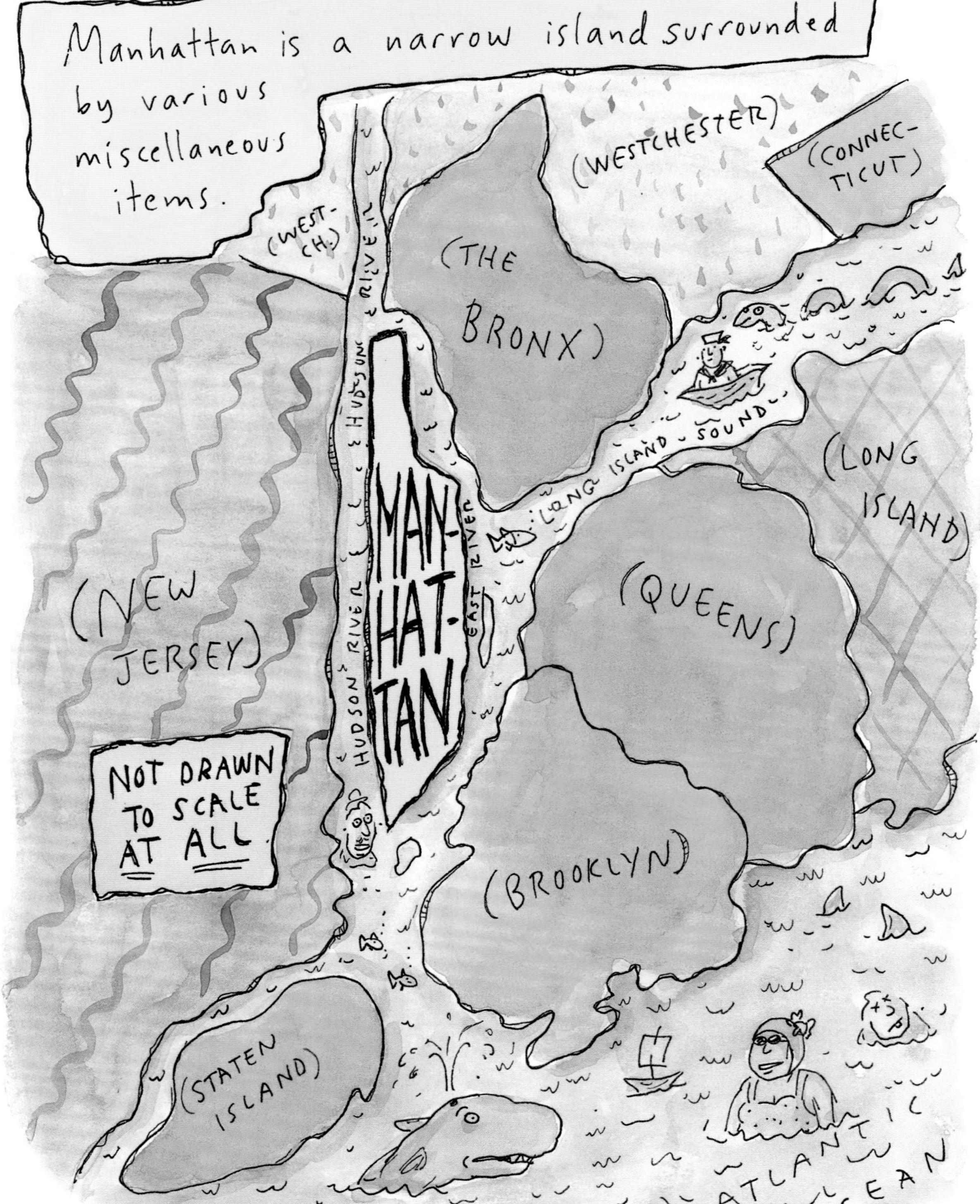
Manhattan is a narrow island surrounded by various miscellaneous items.
(WESTCHESTER)
(CONNEC-TICUT)
(WEST-CH.)
HUDSON RIVER
(THE BRONX)
MAN-HAT-TAN
LONG ISLAND SOUND
(LONG ISLAND)
EAST RIVER
(QUEENS)
(NEW JERSEY)
NOT DRAWN TO SCALE AT ALL
(BROOKLYN)
(STATEN ISLAND)
(THE MIGHTY) ATLANTIC OCEAN

Nearly all of Manhattan is laid out on a grid:

BROADWAY
AVENUE
STREET

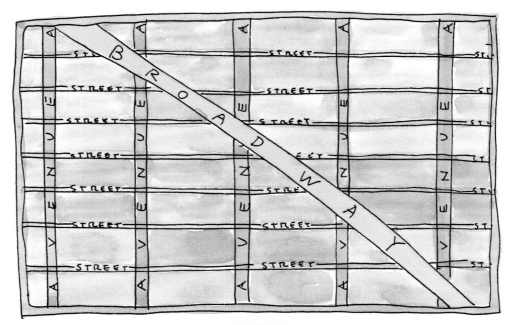

FACTS:

- Avenues run NORTH – SOUTH.
- Streets run EAST – WEST.
- Broadway is the exception. It runs diagonally.
- Avenues are wider than streets, and the distance between avenues is wider than the distance between streets.

HOWEVER:

When you get below 14th Street, especially on the West Side, things get somewhat ungrid-like.

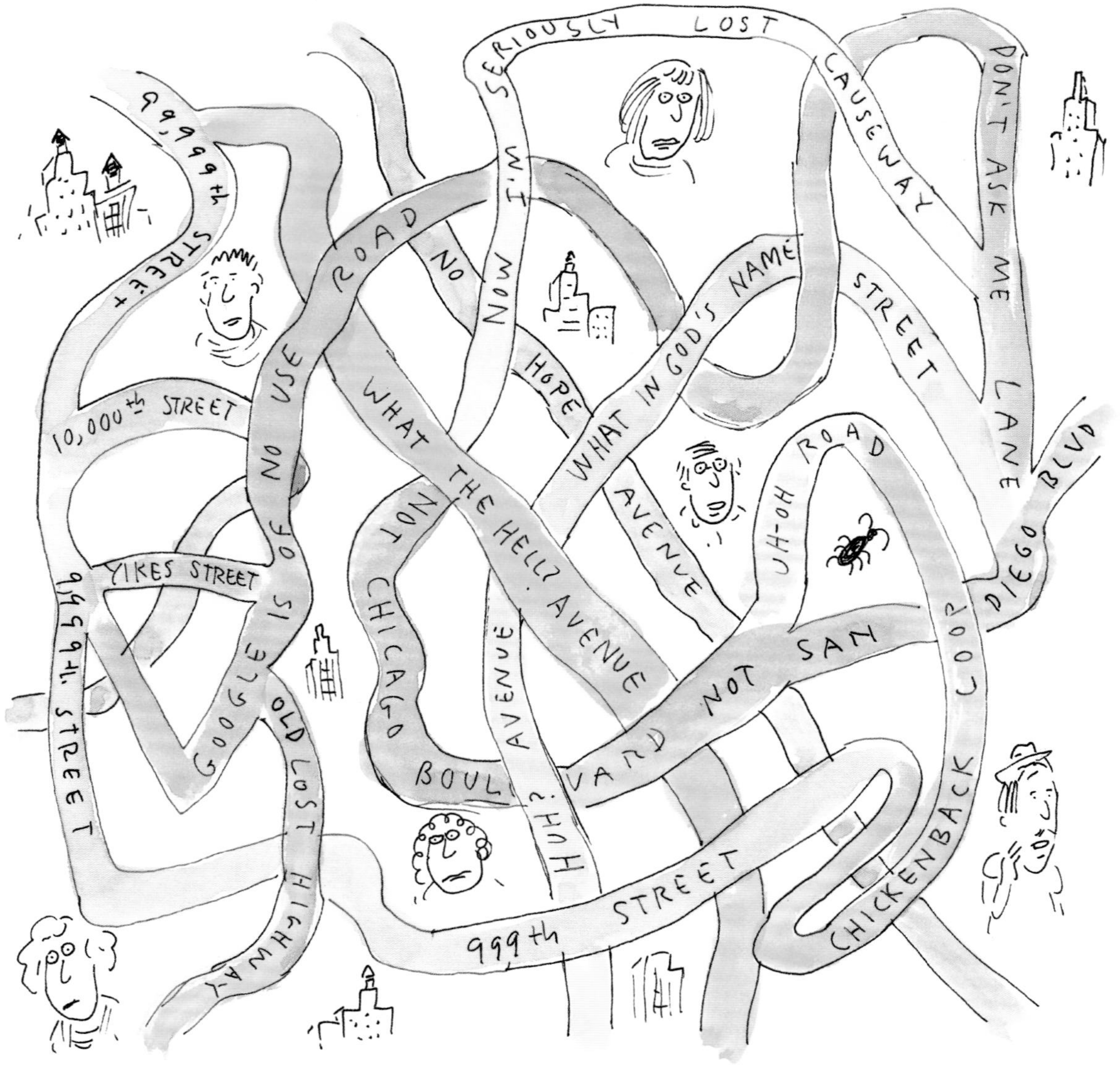

9,999th STREET
SERIOUSLY LOST CAUSEWAY
DON'T ASK ME LANE
I'M NOW NO HOPE
NO USE ROAD
WHAT IN GOD'S NAME STREET
10,000th STREET
YIKES STREET
GOOGLE IS OF
WHAT THE HELL? AVENUE
AVENUE
UH-OH ROAD
DIEGO BLVD
SAN NOT
NOT CHICAGO
CHICAGO BOULEVARD
AVENUE HUH?
9999th STREET
OLD LOST HIGHWAY
999th STREET
CHICKENBACK LOOP

Another important fact:
Fifth Avenue divides the **EAST SIDE** from the **WEST SIDE**.

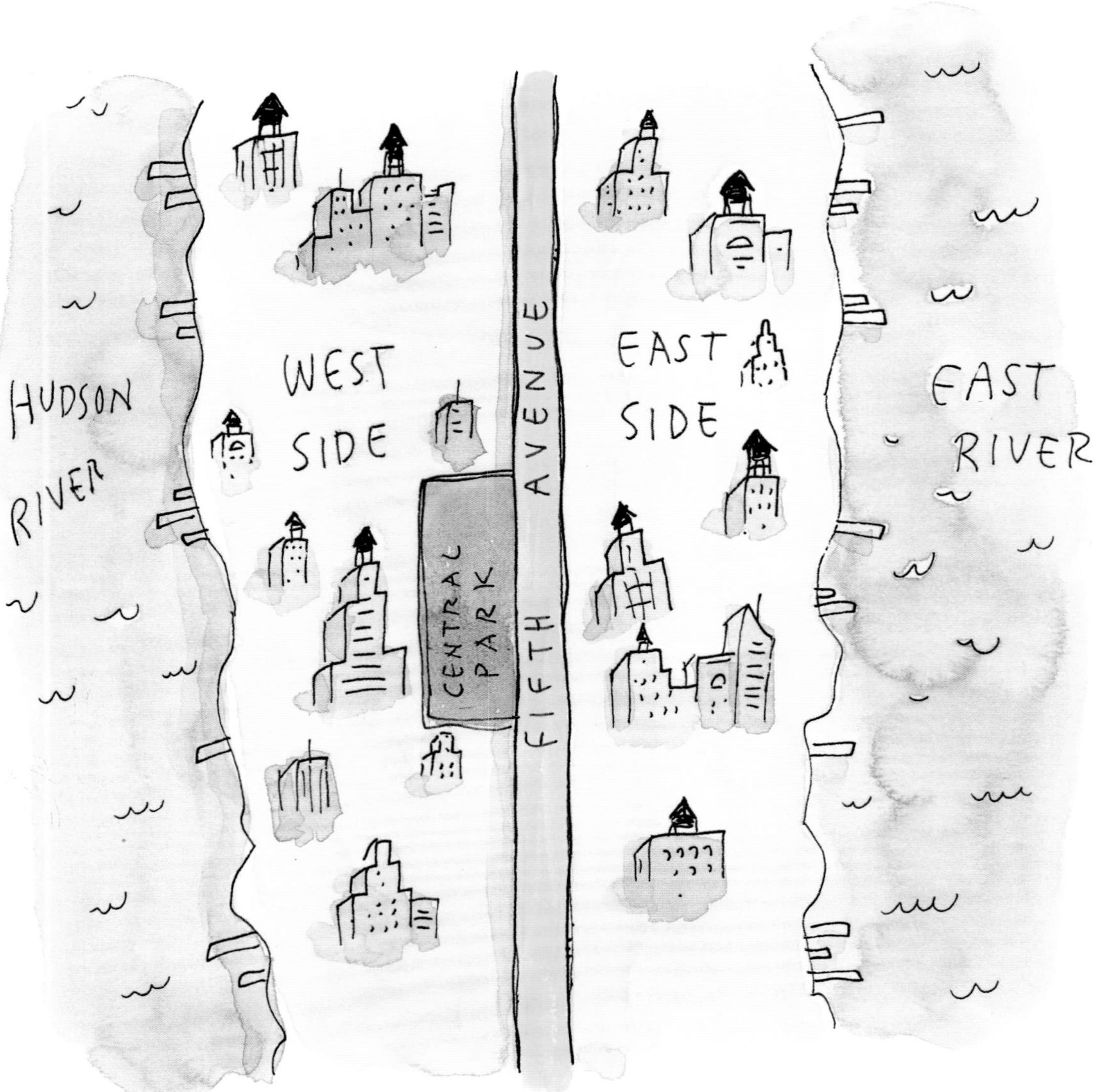

HUDSON RIVER
WEST SIDE
CENTRAL PARK
FIFTH AVENUE
EAST SIDE
EAST RIVER

When looking for a street (not avenue) address, the numbers start at ONE on either side of Fifth Avenue, and increase as you go further east or further west.

What this means is: 25 **WEST** 43rd Street is a completely different building from 25 EAST 43rd Street.

25 WEST 43rd STREET
25 EAST 43rd STREET
WEST 45th
EAST 45th
WEST 44th
EAST 44th
WEST 43rd STREET
EAST 43rd STREET
WEST 42nd
EAST 42nd
WEST 41st
EAST 41st
SIXTH AVENUE
FIFTH AVENUE
MADISON AVENUE

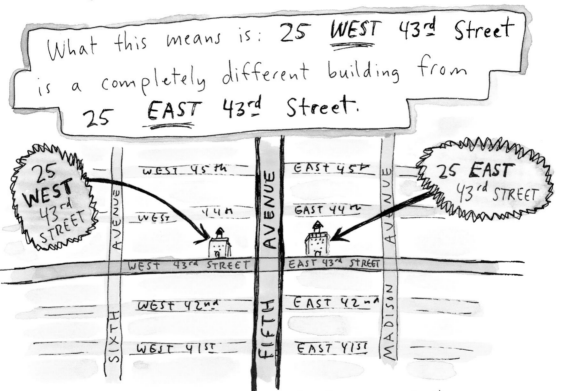

Also: Sixth Avenue and Avenue of the Americas are the same thing. But no one calls it "Avenue of the Americas," because GIVE ME A BREAK.

If the street numbers are going <u>UP</u> (21ST Street, 22nd Street, 23rd Street...) you're heading <u>UPTOWN</u>. *

If the street numbers are going <u>DOWN</u>, (21ST Street, 20th Street, 19th Street...) you're heading <u>DOWNTOWN</u>. **

* UPTOWN can also mean The Bronx.
** DOWNTOWN may mean Brooklyn. That's mainly when you're on the subway. ***
*** Don't worry about that now.

REMEMBER THAT OLD SONG?

♫. New York, New York...

...It's a hell of a town...

The Bronx is up...

...and the Battery's down...

...and so is Brooklyn...

...and what about Queens...

The best thing about Manhattan's grid-like design is, you can't get too lost.

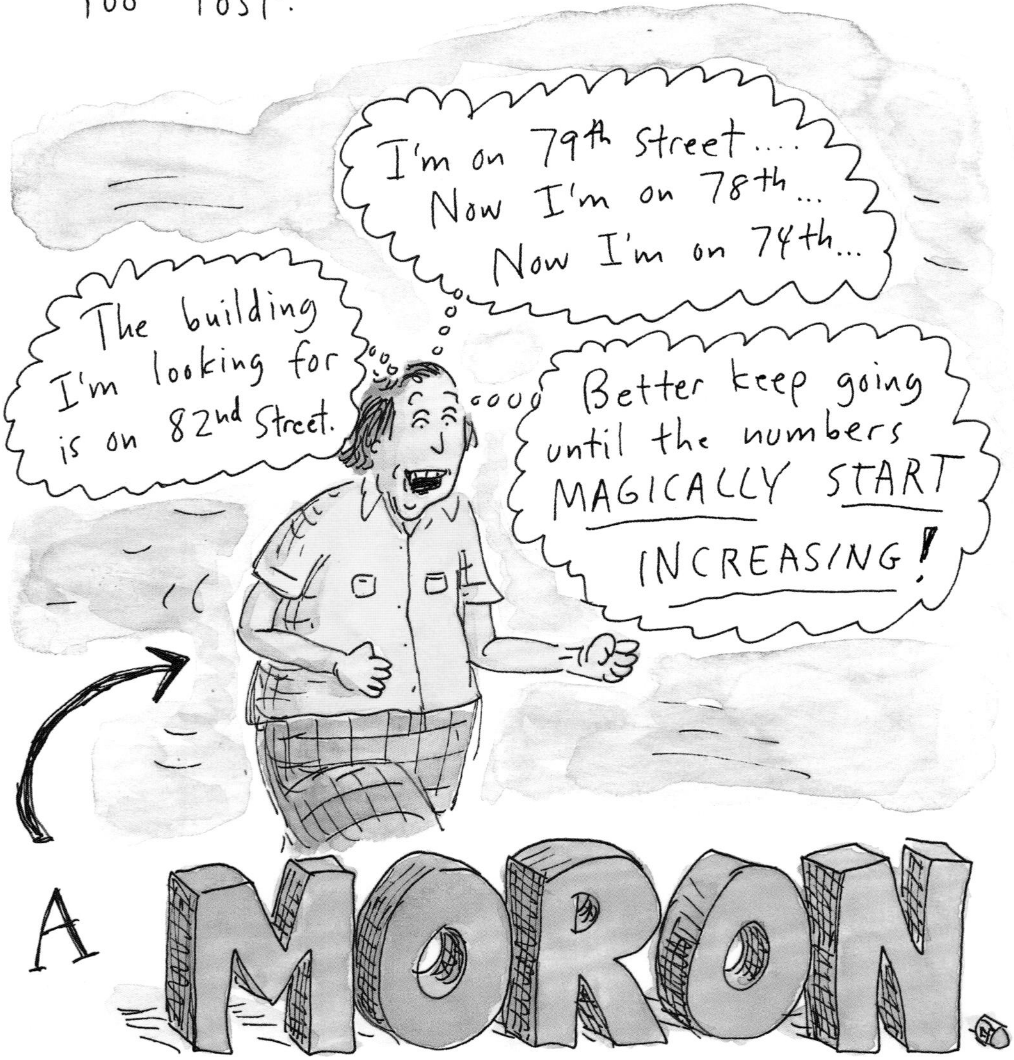
I'm on 79th street....
Now I'm on 78th...
Now I'm on 74th...
The building I'm looking for is on 82nd Street.
Better keep going until the numbers MAGICALLY START INCREASING!
A MORON.

A term you're going to hear a lot is

CROSS-STREET.

For example:

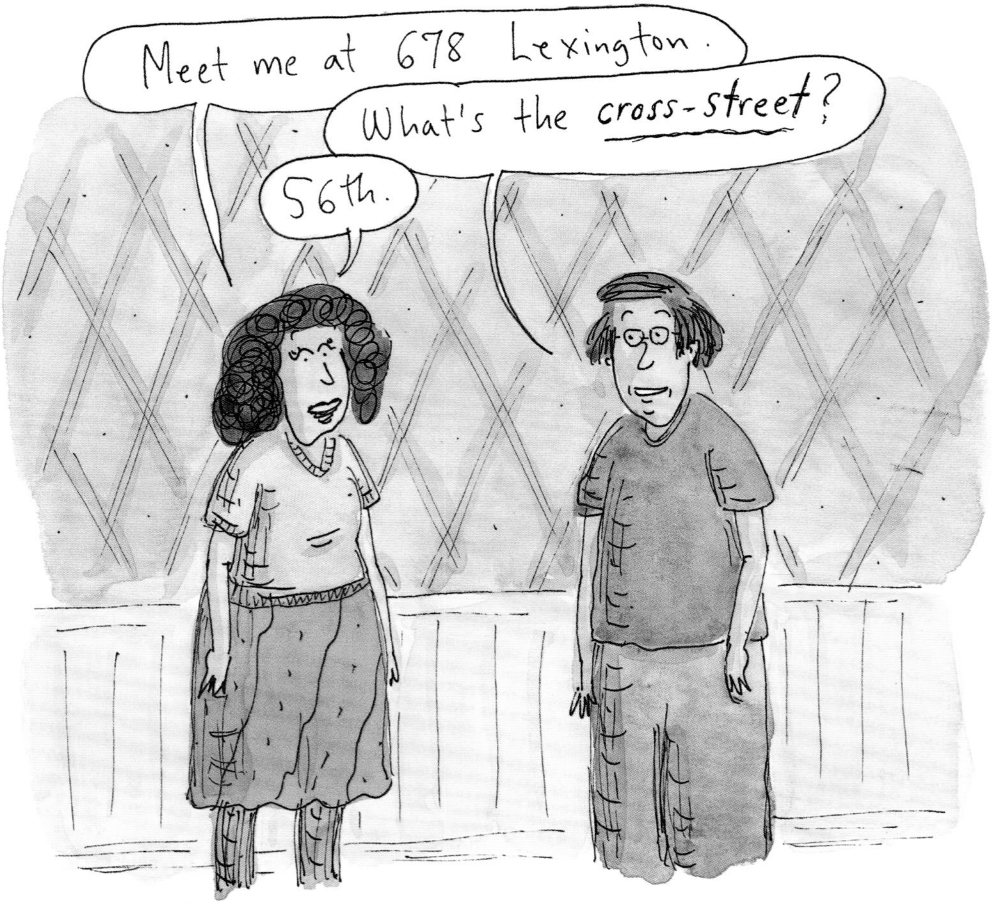

Meet me at 678 Lexington.
What's the cross-street?
56th.

Perhaps you are wondering:

WHAT IS A CROSS-STREET?

A cross-street is simply the number of the street that intersects whatever avenue you're on.

WEST 78th STREET
YOU
WEST 77th STREET
WEST 76th STREET
WEST 75th STREET
AMSTERDAM AVENUE

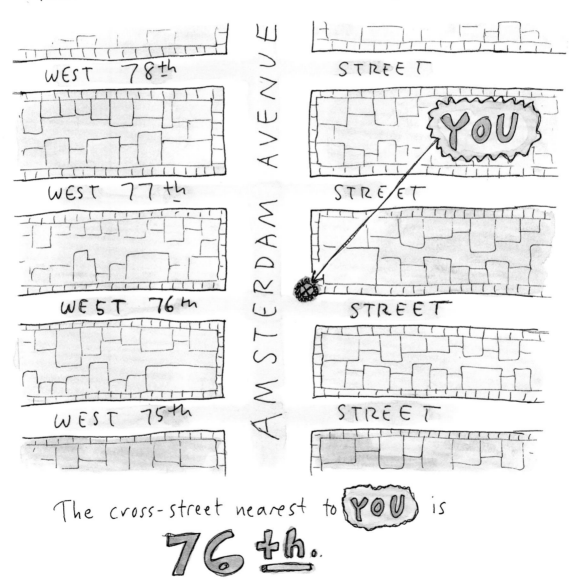

The cross-street nearest to YOU is

76th.

If all you have is an avenue address, find out the cross-street, or you're going to be wandering around like a lost Swedish tourist.

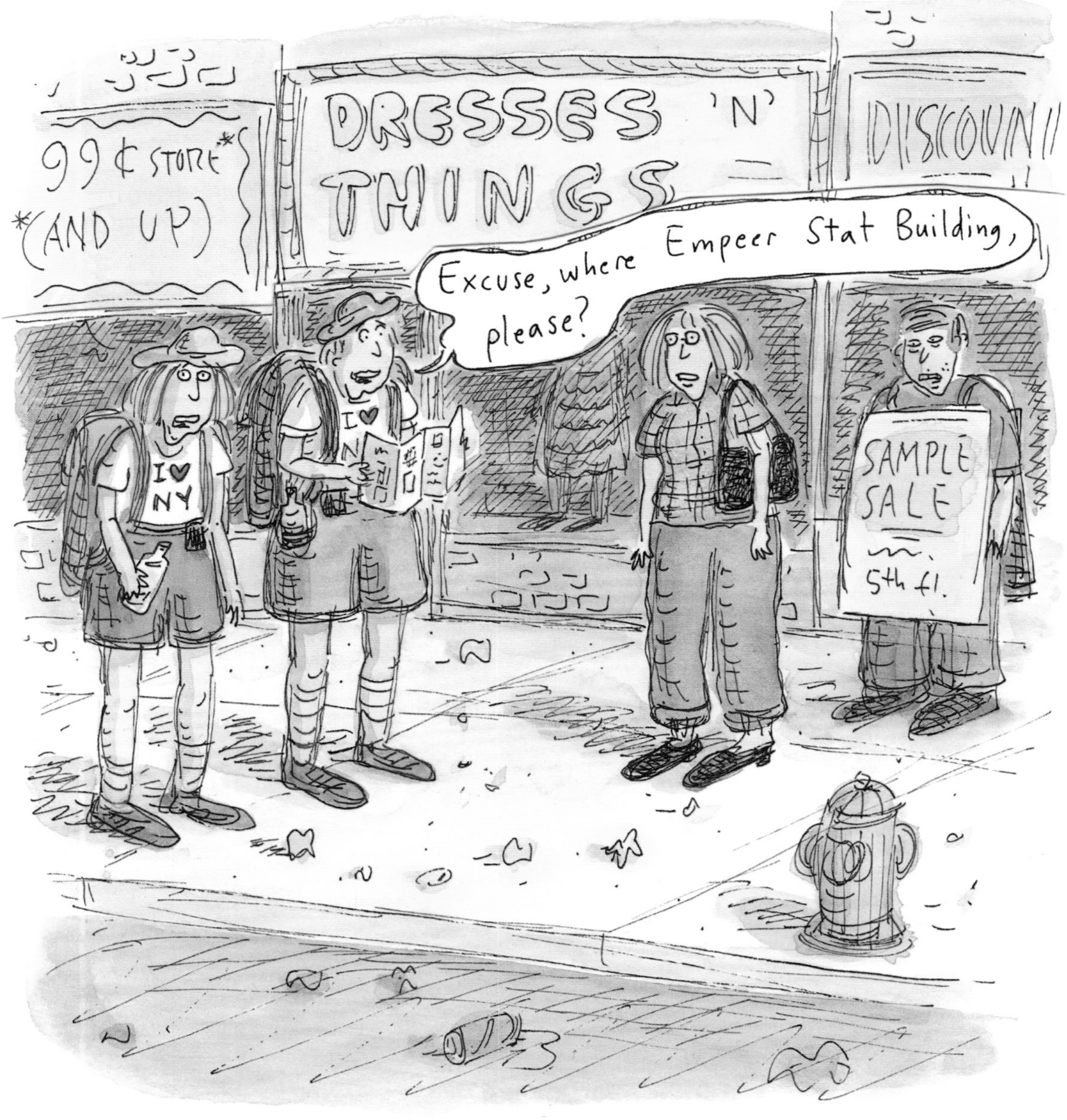
99¢ STORE*
*(AND UP)
DRESSES 'N' THINGS
DISCOUN
Excuse, where Empeer Stat Building, please?
I ♥ NY
SAMPLE SALE
5th fl.

There are various formulas for working out the cross-street:

Just take the address...

Divide by six...

Find the square root...

Add either 17 or 52 or 93, depending on whether it's before or after noon...

But what year is this, 1978? No. Look it up on your phone.

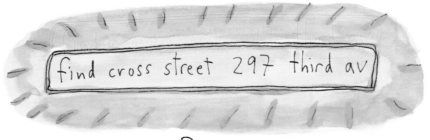

find cross street 297 third av

Done.

The best way to get acquainted with the layout of the city is to **WALK AROUND**. To a great extent, everything in Manhattan is within walking distance of everything else. Between walking, biking, subways, buses, taxis, Uber-type apps, and everything else, who needs a stupid car?

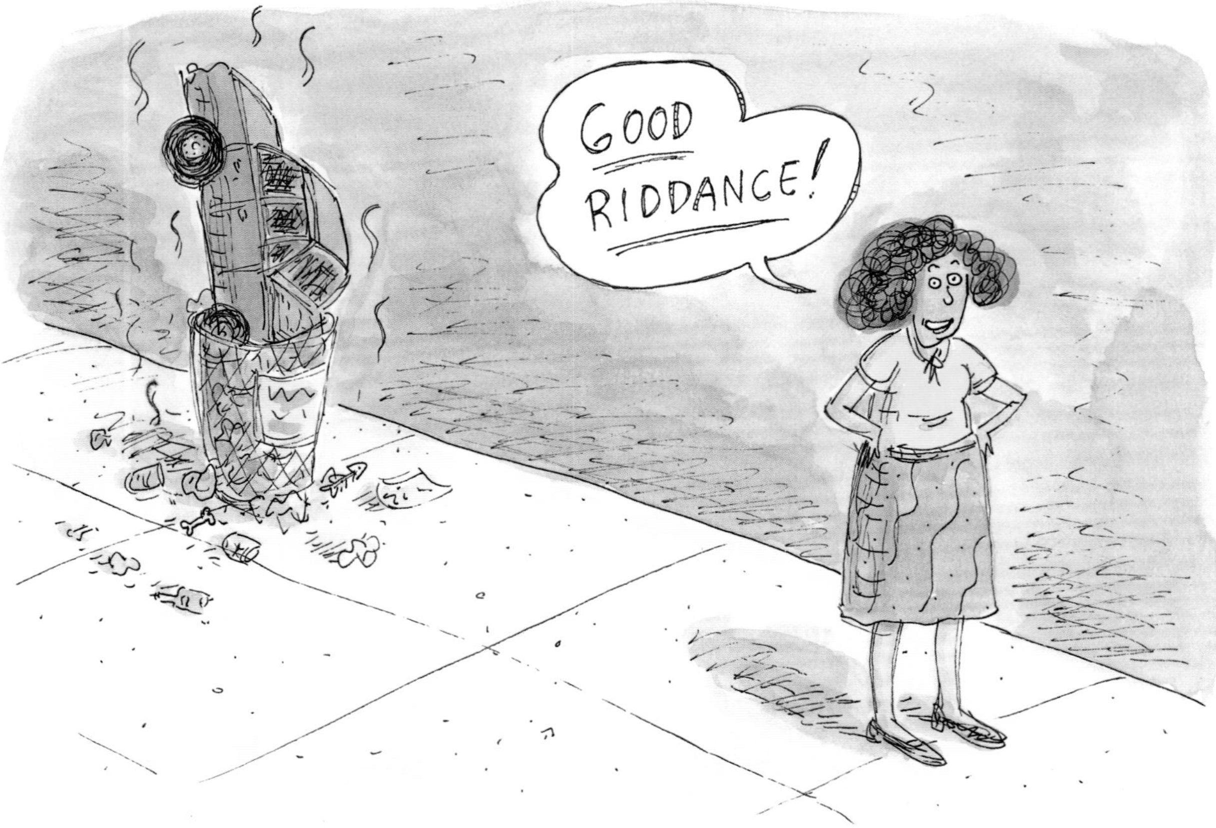
GOOD RIDDANCE!

3

WALKING AROUND

One of the greatest things you can do in life is walk around New York. Nature is great, but at a certain point, the mind wanders.

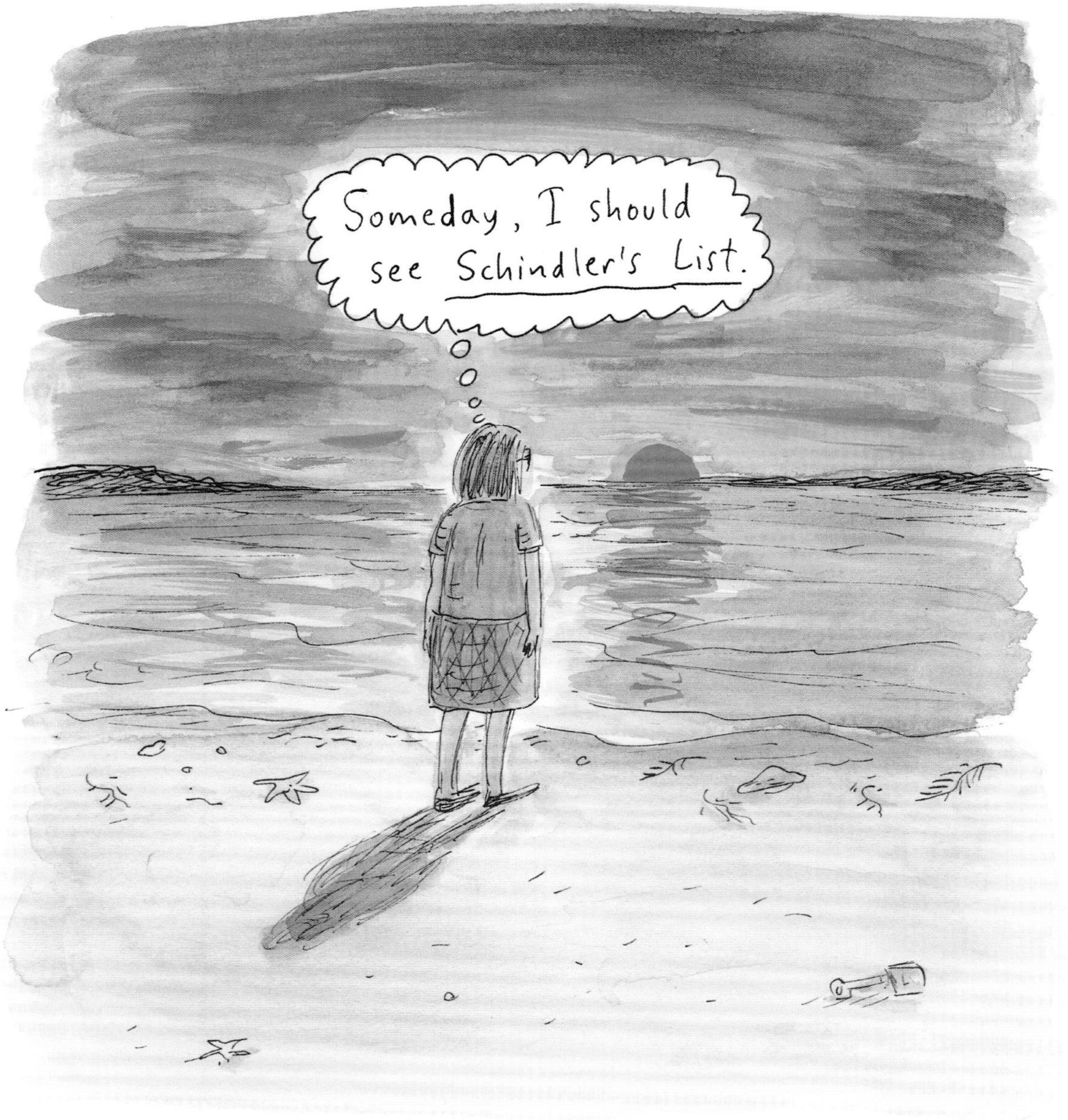
Someday, I should see Schindler's List.

For some reason, I've always preferred cities to Nature. I am interested in the person-made. I like to watch and eavesdrop on people. And I really like DENSITY OF VISUAL INFORMATION.

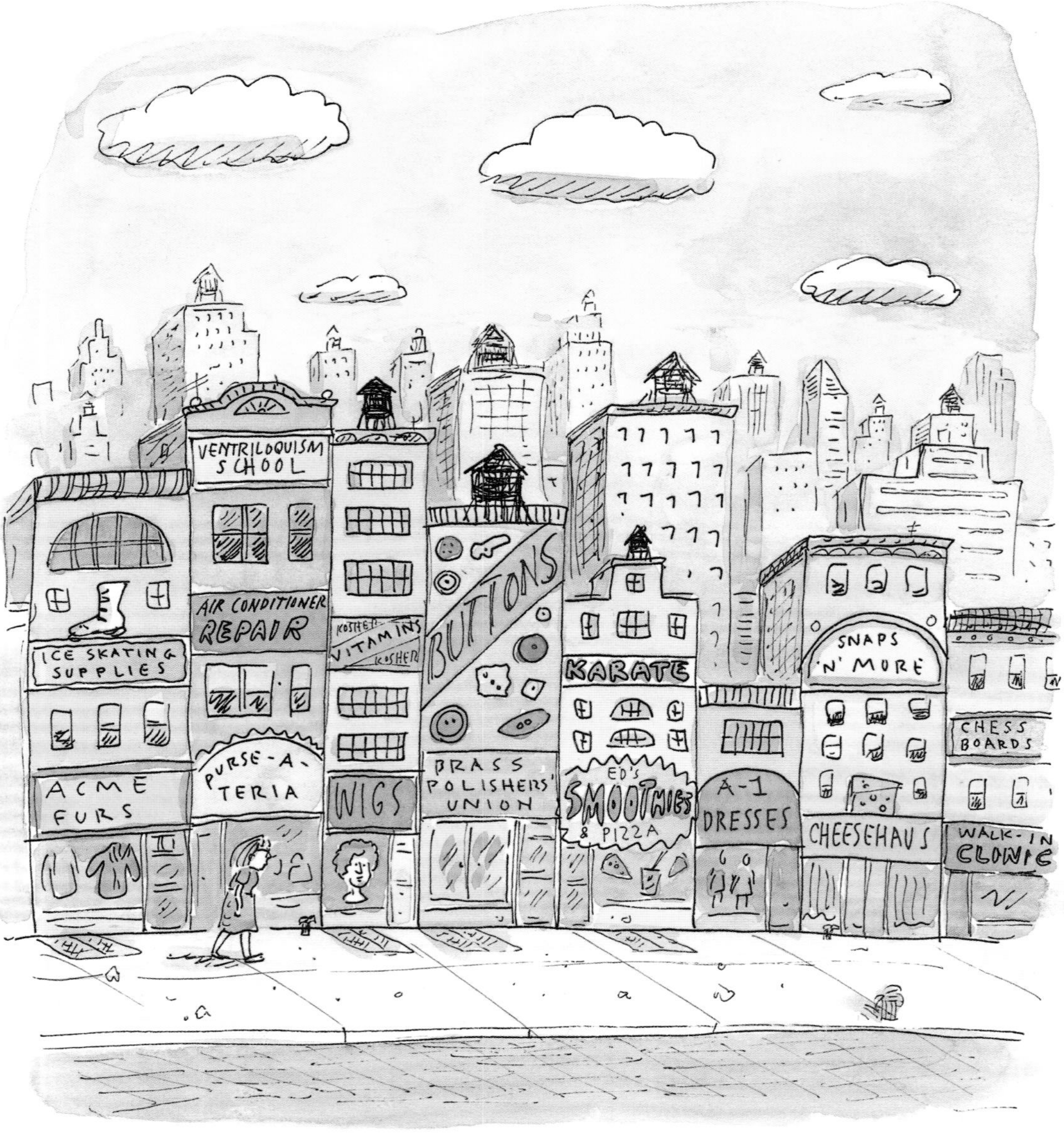
VENTRILOQUISM SCHOOL
AIR CONDITIONER REPAIR
ICE SKATING SUPPLIES
KOSHER VITAMINS KOSHER
BUTTONS
KARATE
SNAPS 'N' MORE
CHESS BOARDS
ACME FURS
PURSE-A-TERIA
WIGS
BRASS POLISHERS' UNION
ED'S SMOOTHIES & PIZZA
A-1 DRESSES
CHEESEHAUS
WALK-IN CLINIC

Pick a random building in New York, examine it from top to bottom, and this is what you might see:

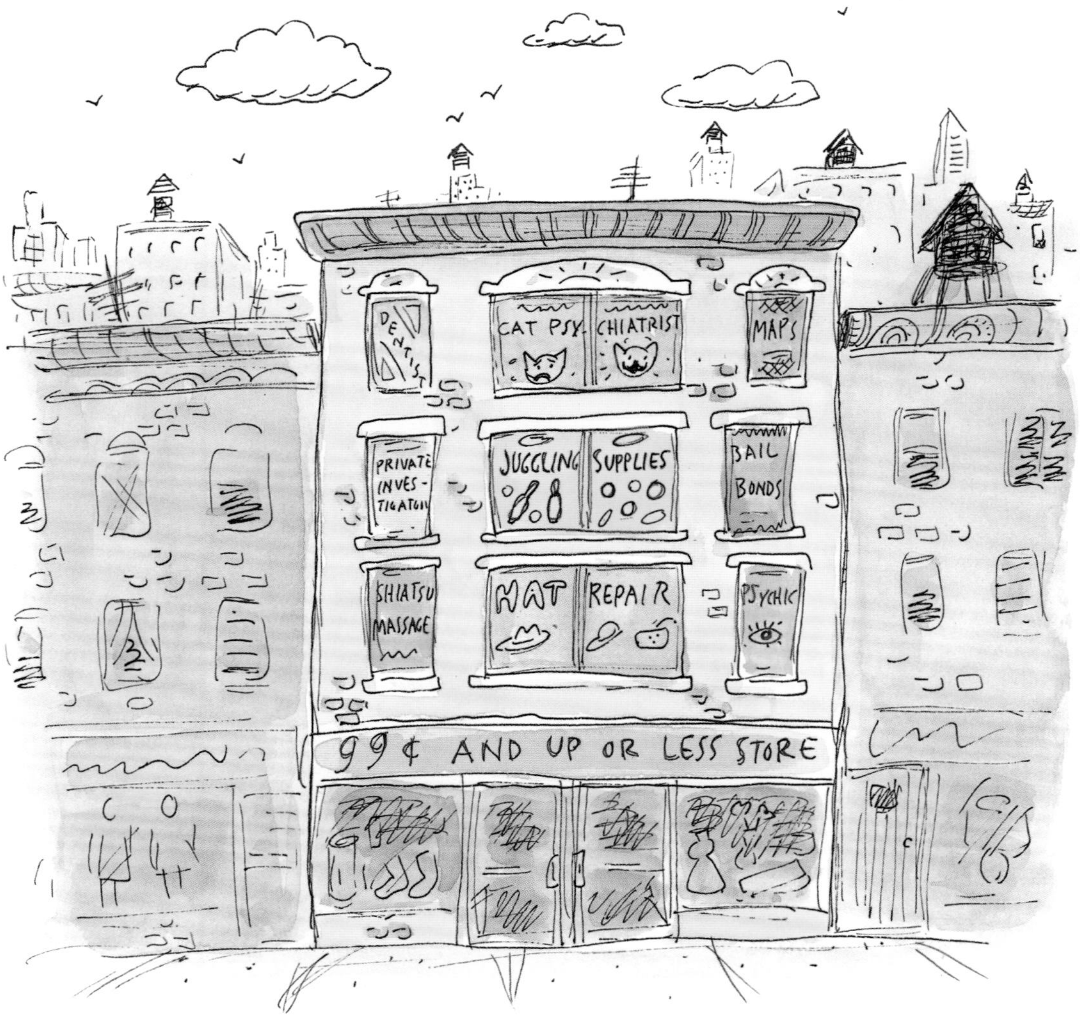

DENTIST
CAT PSYCHIATRIST
MAPS
PRIVATE INVESTIGATION
JUGGLING SUPPLIES
BAIL BONDS
SHIATSU MASSAGE
HAT REPAIR
PSYCHIC
99¢ AND UP OR LESS STORE

I don't know why that makes me happy to look at, but it does.

As I mentioned before, New York is one of the few places where having a car is more of a hindrance than an advantage. Walking is often the quickest and most interesting way to get around.

Also, in almost every other city, at least in the U.S., if you're in the downtown area in the middle of the afternoon, the streets will be **EMPTY**.

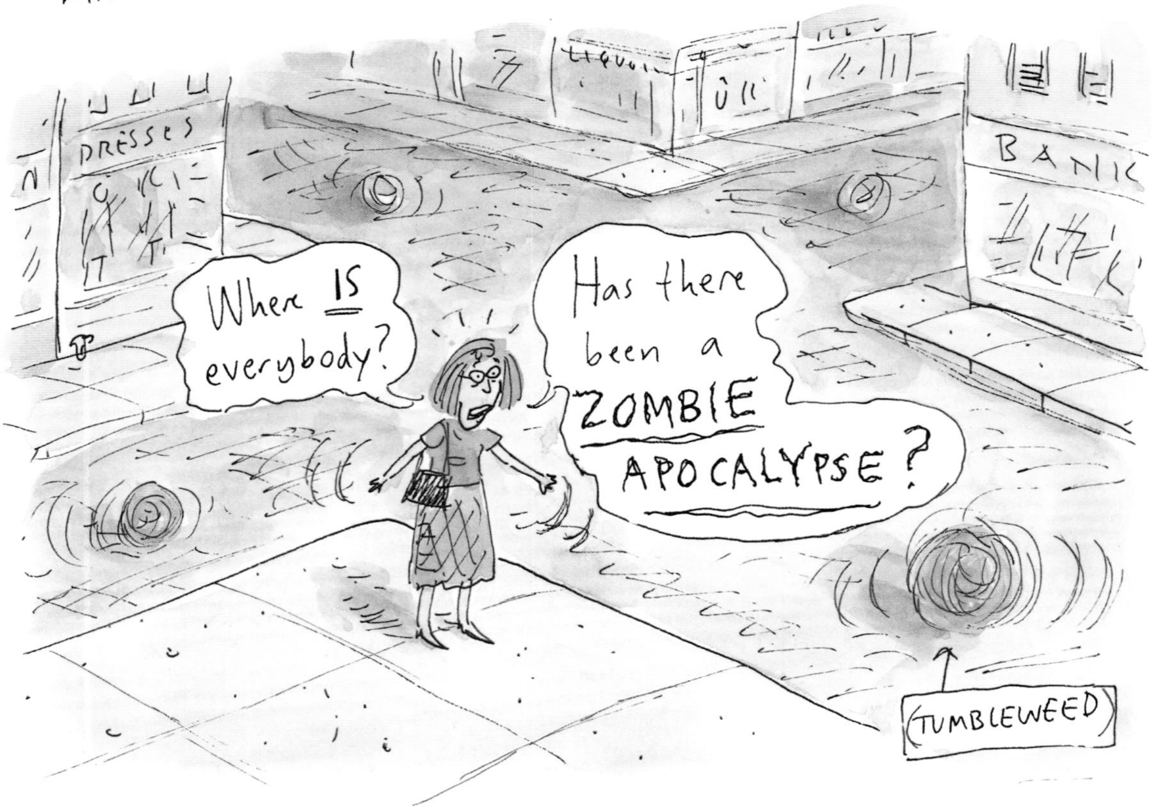
DRESSES
BANK
Where IS everybody?
Has there been a ZOMBIE APOCALYPSE?
TUMBLEWEED

One of the reasons for that is that most U.S. cities are too spread out.

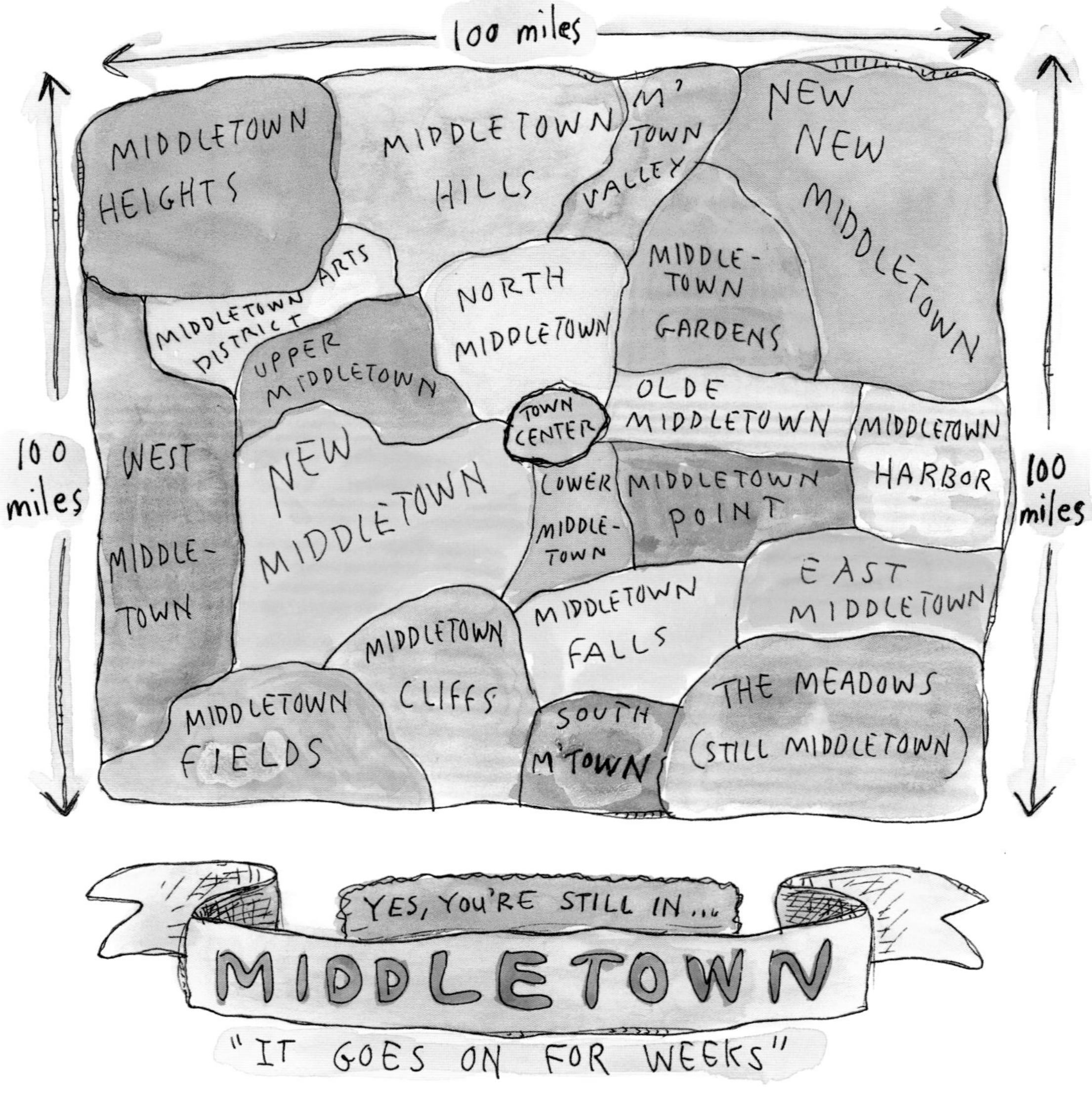
100 miles
100 miles
100 miles
MIDDLETOWN HEIGHTS
MIDDLETOWN HILLS
M'TOWN VALLEY
NEW NEW MIDDLETOWN
MIDDLETOWN ARTS DISTRICT
NORTH MIDDLETOWN
MIDDLE-TOWN GARDENS
UPPER MIDDLETOWN
OLDE MIDDLETOWN
TOWN CENTER
MIDDLETOWN HARBOR
WEST MIDDLE-TOWN
NEW MIDDLETOWN
LOWER MIDDLE-TOWN
MIDDLETOWN POINT
EAST MIDDLETOWN
MIDDLETOWN CLIFFS
MIDDLETOWN FALLS
MIDDLETOWN FIELDS
SOUTH M'TOWN
THE MEADOWS (STILL MIDDLETOWN)
YES, YOU'RE STILL IN...
MIDDLETOWN
"IT GOES ON FOR WEEKS"

In Manhattan, especially in Midtown, the streets are rarely empty. The main drawback is getting stuck in a herd of out-of-towners who, for some reason, always seem reluctant to cross against the light.

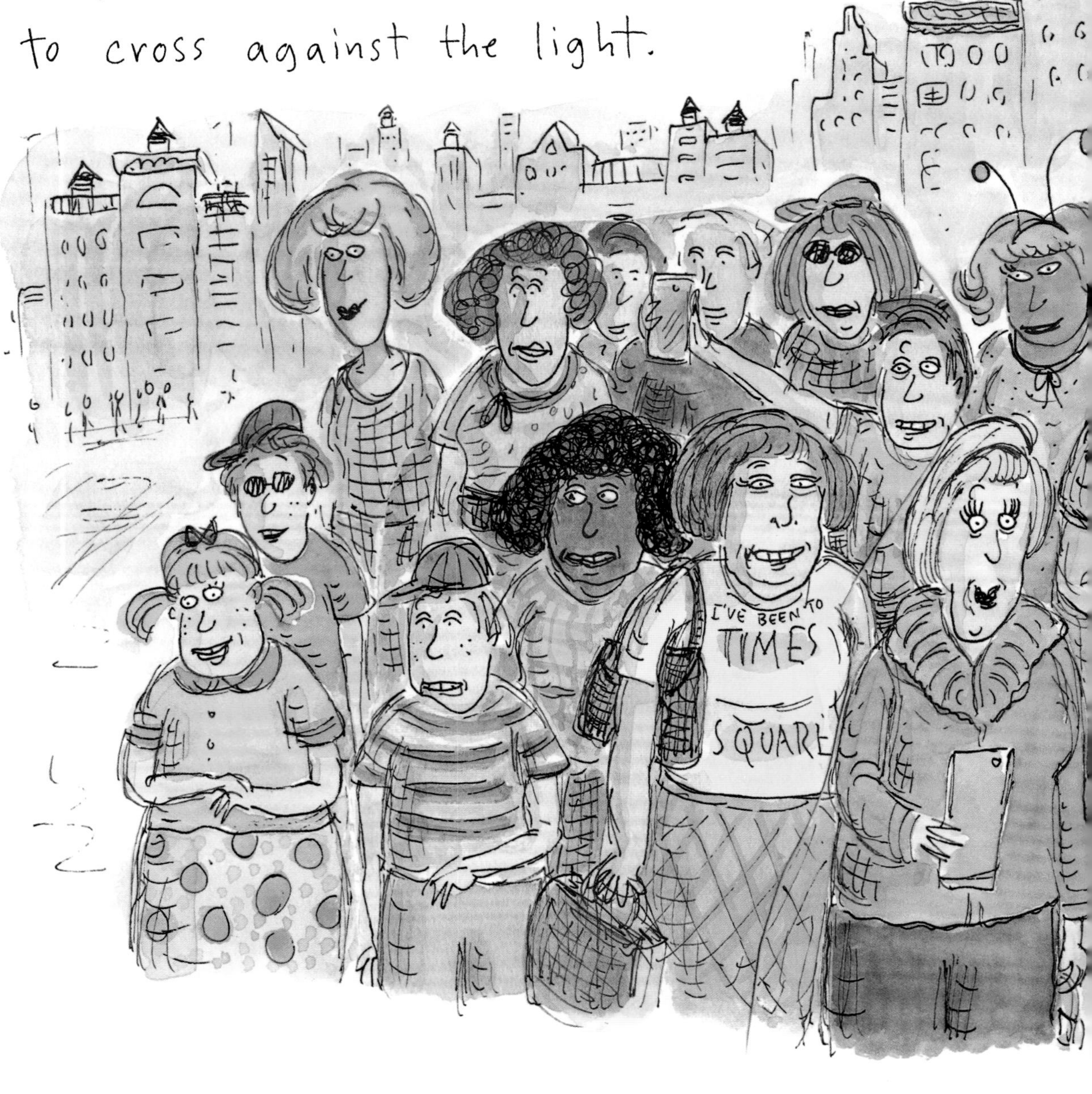
I'VE BEEN TO TIMES SQUARE

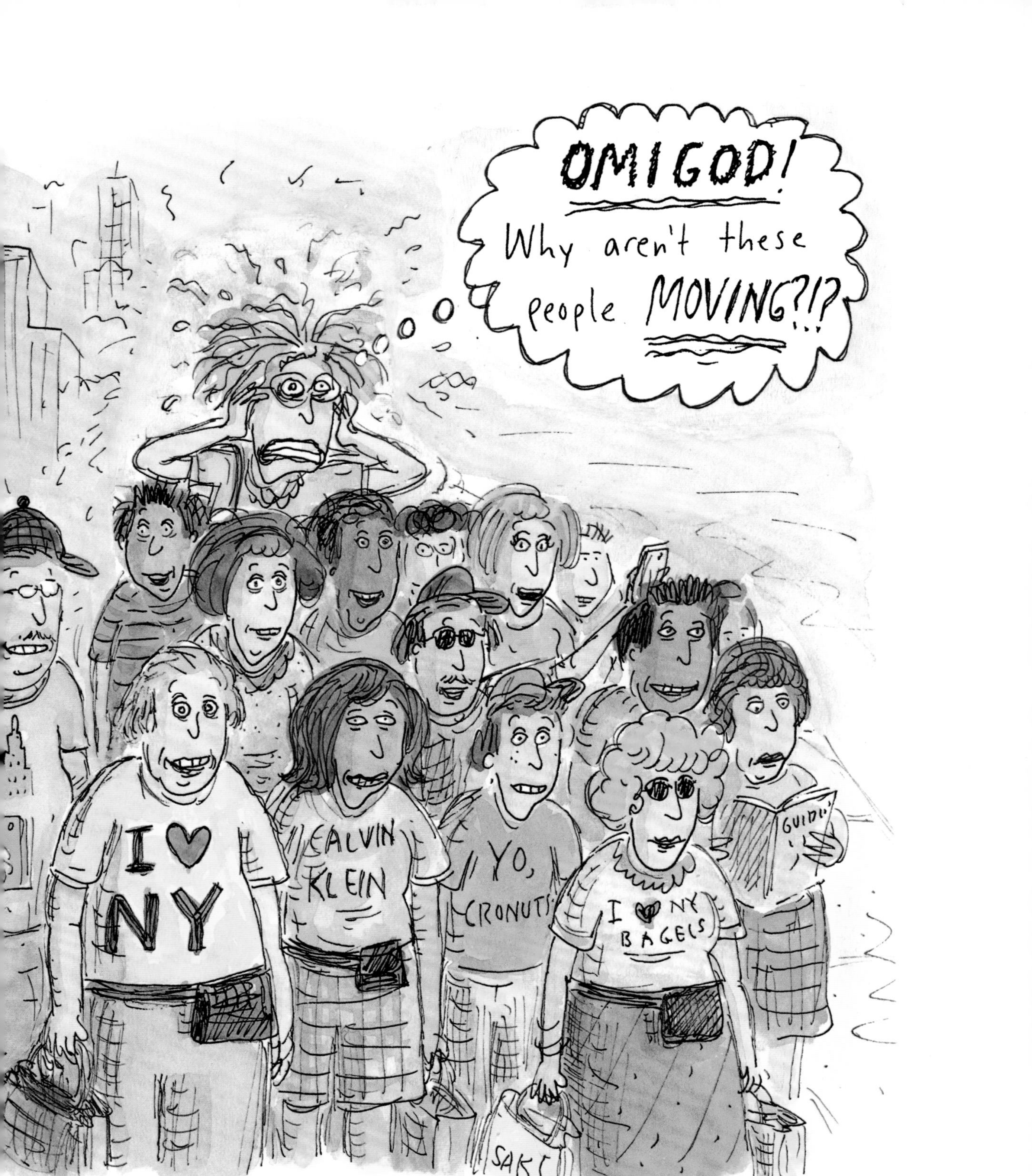
OMIGOD!
Why aren't these people MOVING?!?
I ♥ NY
CALVIN KLEIN
YO, CRONUTS
I ♥ NY BAGELS
GUIDE
SAKS

At its widest, Manhattan is only 2.3 miles across.
You could probably plug in a toaster in an apartment
near the Hudson River, run the cord along 14th Street,
and make yourself some toast near the East River.

Not that you'd <u>want</u> to do this. Just saying, if you *did*,
it wouldn't be all that difficult.

If you are feeling antsy or out of sorts, pick a street and walk across it from coast to coast. Any street will do.

WEAR COMFORTABLE SHOES

The more nondescript your street is, the greater

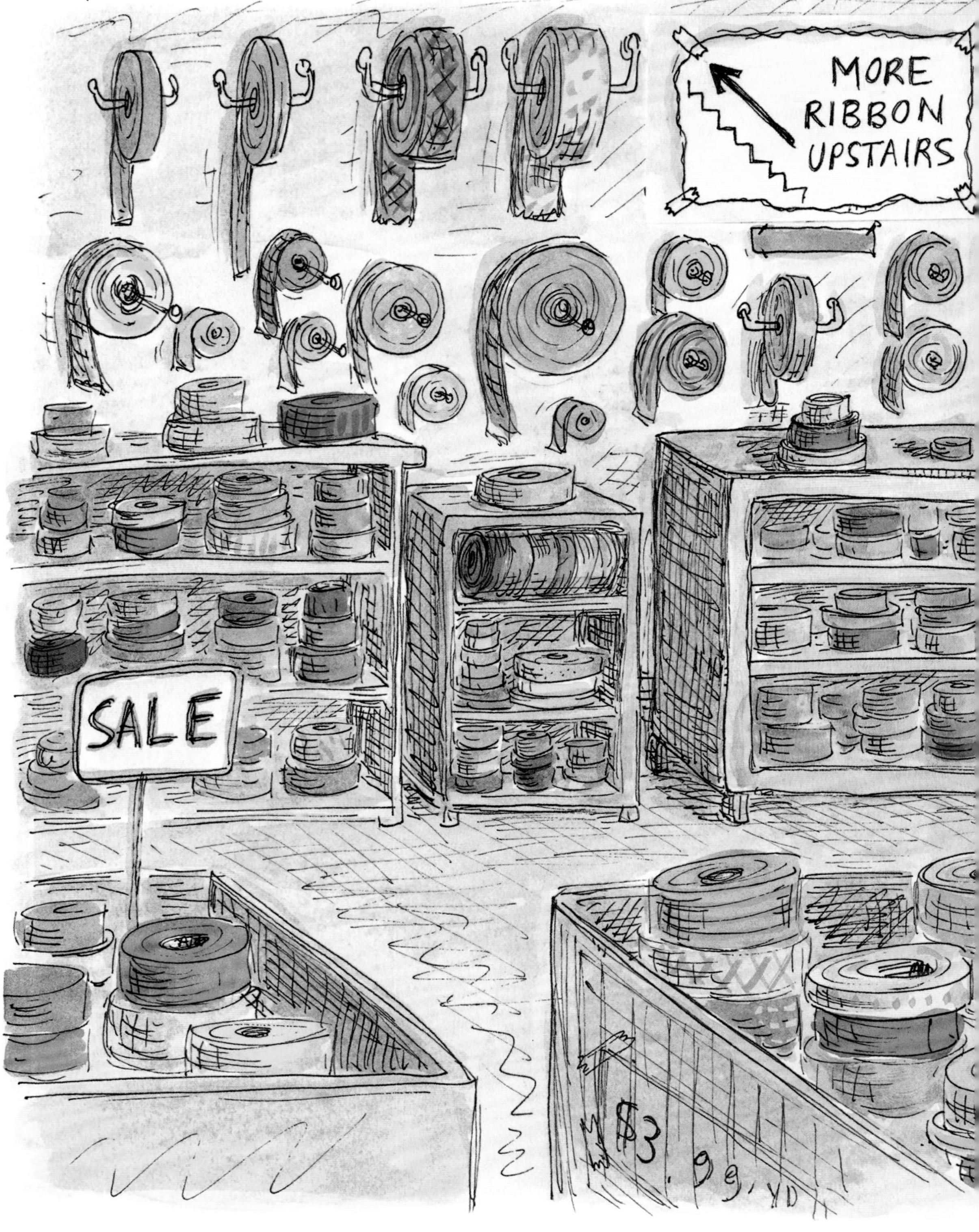
MORE
RIBBON
UPSTAIRS
SALE
$3.99/YD

chance you have of making your own discoveries.

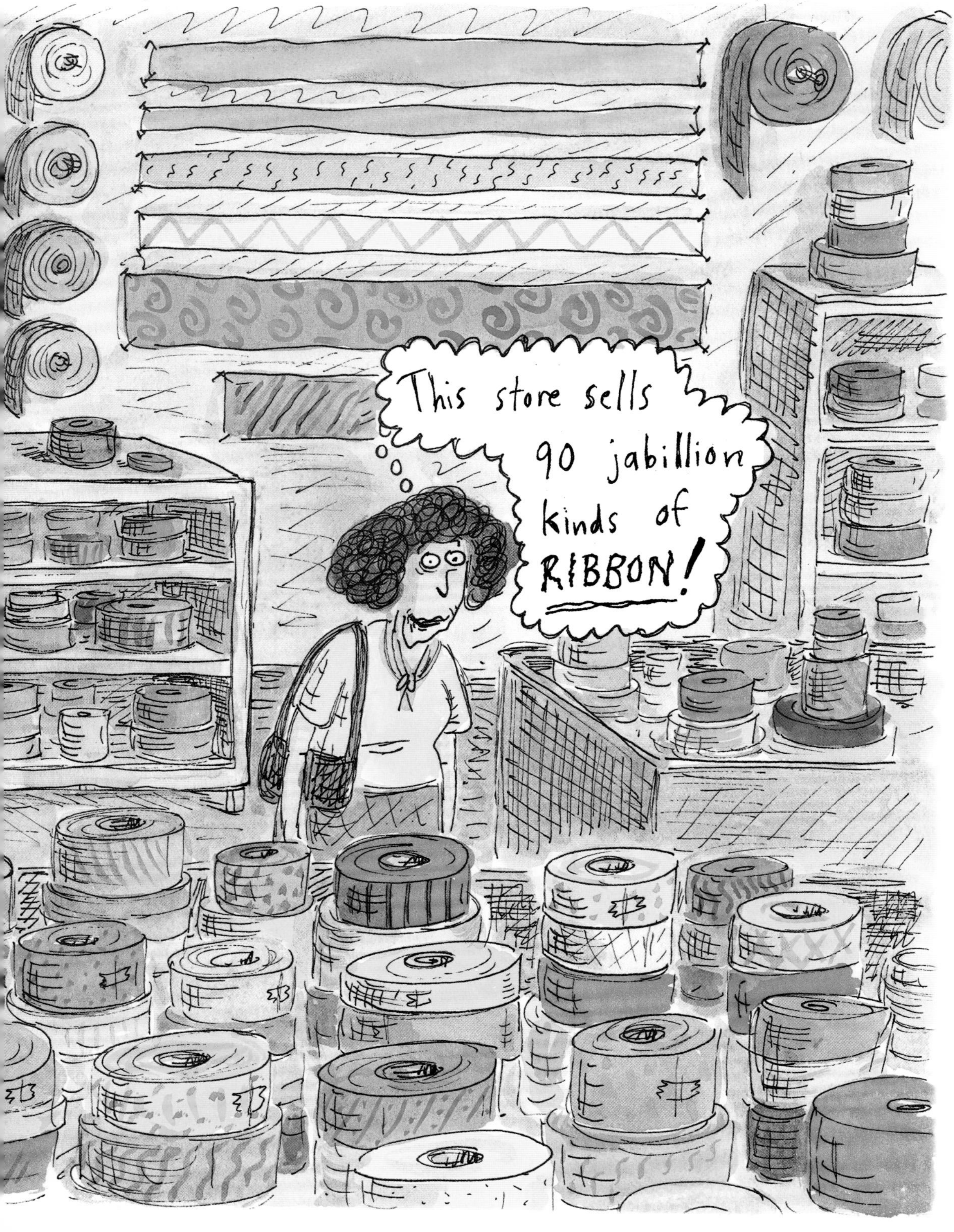
This store sells 90 jabillion kinds of RIBBON!

When you walk around, keep your eyes and ears open. Partly for safety - you don't want to get smashed by a bus - but also because there's _SO_ _MUCH_

MATERIAL.

The people, the buildings, things expected, things unexpected, or something surprising you might find on the sidewalk right in front of you. Not money or dog poop or a dead body. Something **REALLY** surprising...

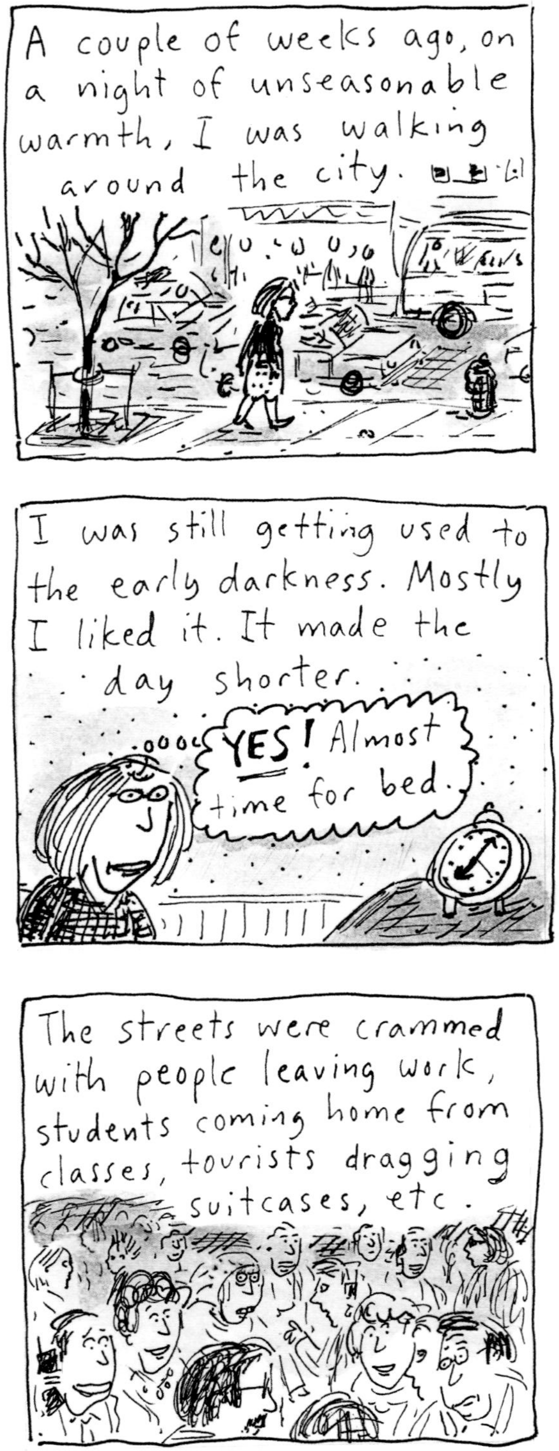
A couple of weeks ago, on a night of unseasonable warmth, I was walking around the city.
I was still getting used to the early darkness. Mostly I liked it. It made the day shorter.
YES! Almost time for bed.
The streets were crammed with people leaving work, students coming home from classes, tourists dragging suitcases, etc.

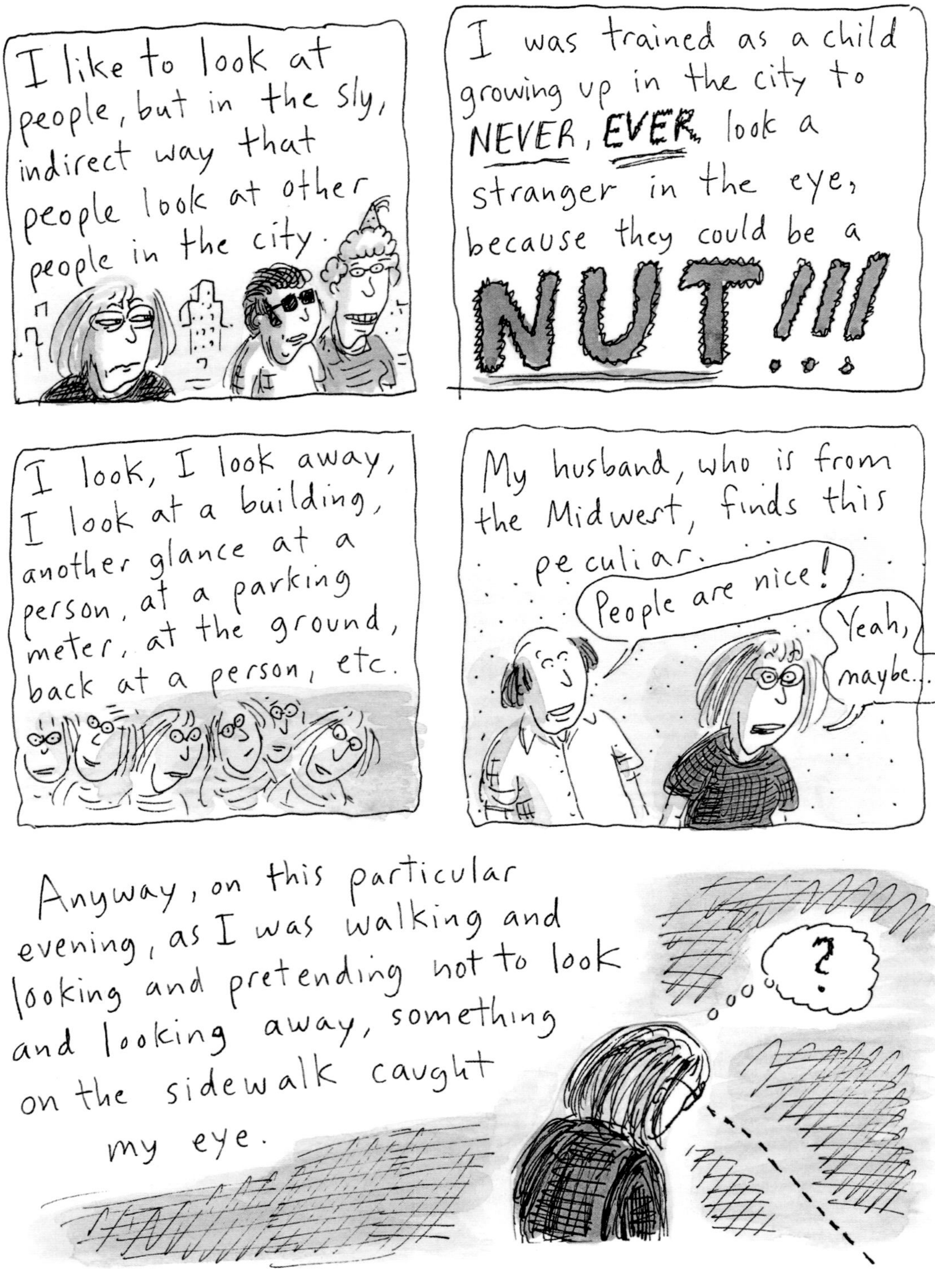
I like to look at people, but in the sly, indirect way that people look at other people in the city.
I was trained as a child growing up in the city to NEVER, EVER look a stranger in the eye, because they could be a
NUT!!!
I look, I look away, I look at a building, another glance at a person, at a parking meter, at the ground, back at a person, etc.
My husband, who is from the Midwest, finds this peculiar.
People are nice!
Yeah, maybe...
Anyway, on this particular evening, as I was walking and looking and pretending not to look and looking away, something on the sidewalk caught my eye.
?

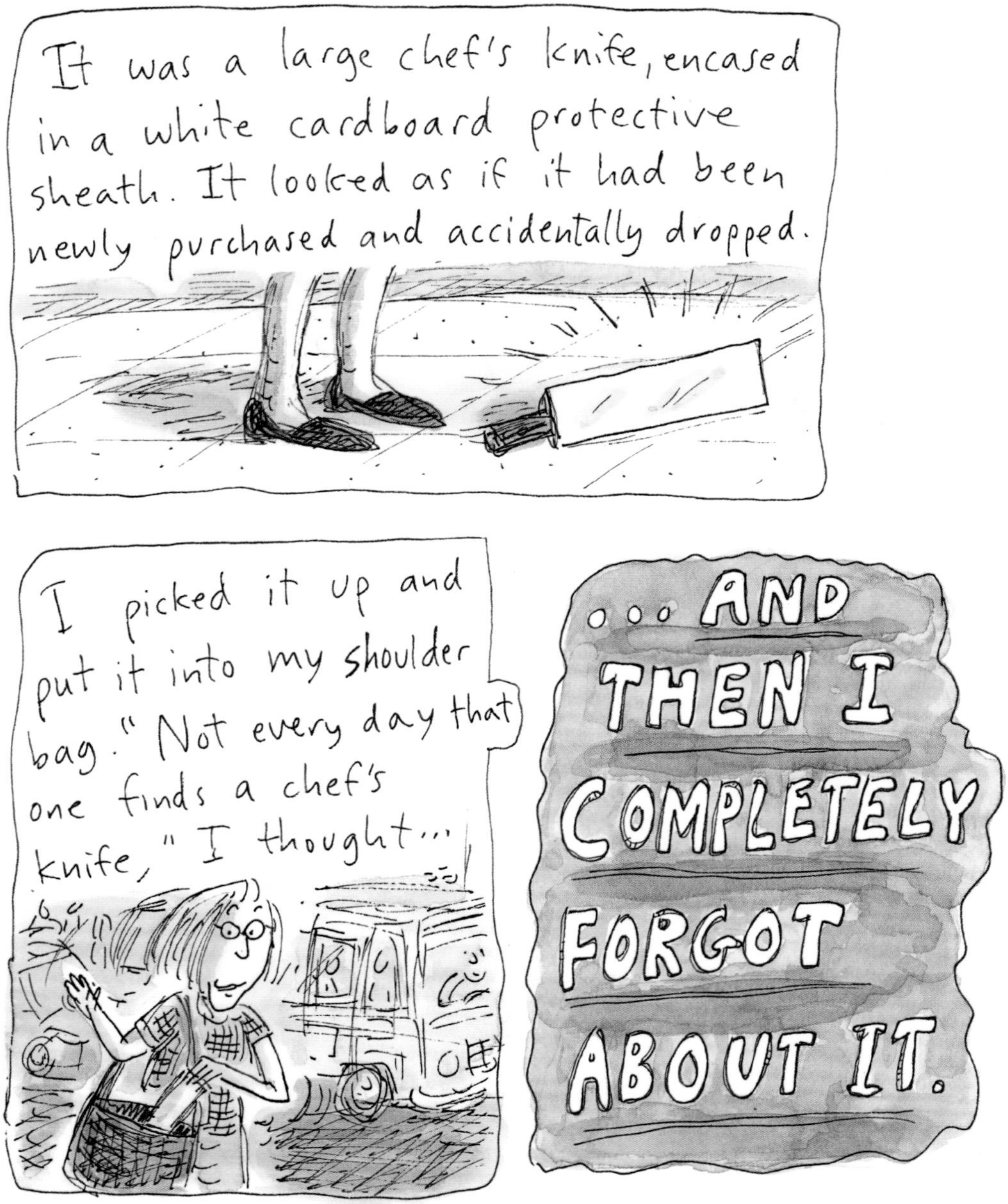
It was a large chef's knife, encased in a white cardboard protective sheath. It looked as if it had been newly purchased and accidentally dropped.
I picked it up and put it into my shoulder bag. "Not every day that one finds a chef's knife," I thought...
...AND THEN I COMPLETELY FORGOT ABOUT IT.

I kept walking. I wasn't tired, and the city was filled with wonderful distractions.
USED BOOKS
ART SUPPLIES
SALE
DELI
HAM & CHEESE WARPS
I met my daughter for dinner at an Italian restaurant.
We ate and drank and yakked for a long time.
It was such a nice night that after dinner, we started walking uptown.
I have a BRAINSTORM! Let's go to the top of the EMPIRE STATE BUILDING!!
O.K.!!!

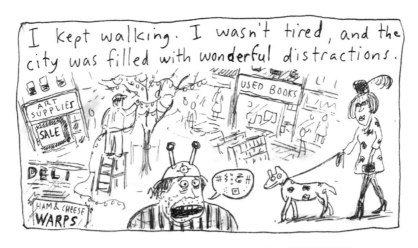

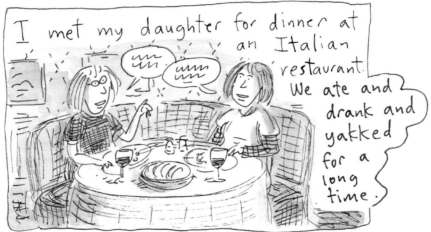

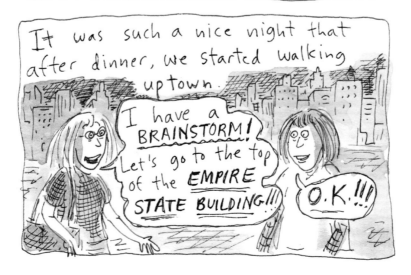

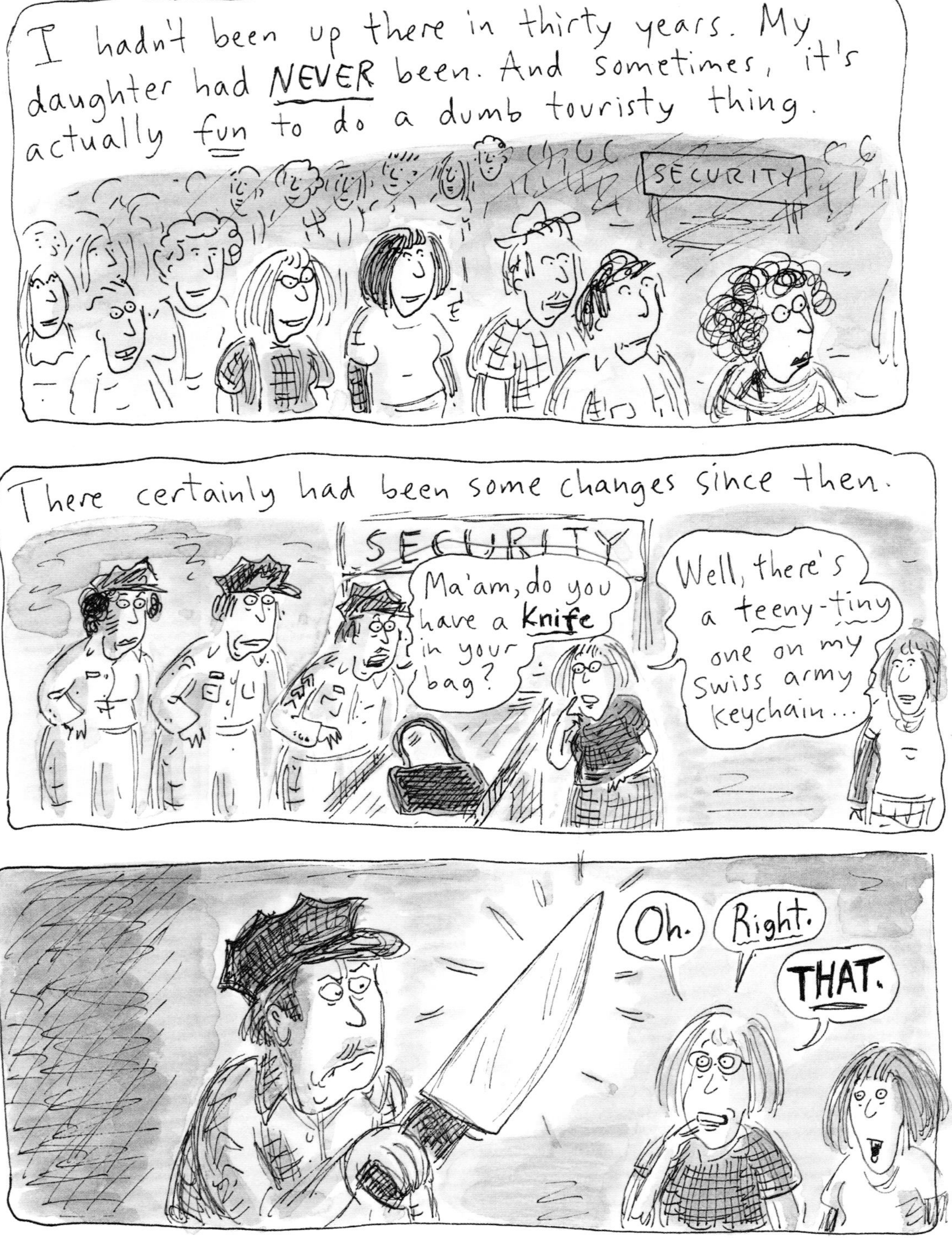
I hadn't been up there in thirty years. My daughter had NEVER been. And sometimes, it's actually fun to do a dumb touristy thing.
SECURITY
There certainly had been some changes since then.
SECURITY
Ma'am, do you have a knife in your bag?
Well, there's a teeny-tiny one on my Swiss army keychain...
Oh.
Right.
THAT.

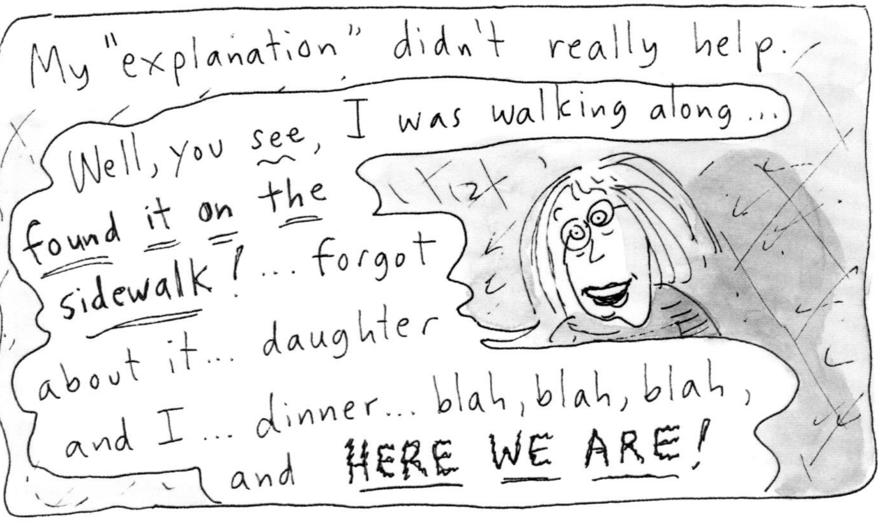
My "explanation" didn't really help.
Well, you see, I was walking along... found it on the sidewalk!... forgot about it... daughter and I... dinner... blah, blah, blah, and HERE WE ARE!

They believed me, but they confiscated it and said I could reclaim it when we came back down from the observation deck. I never bothered.

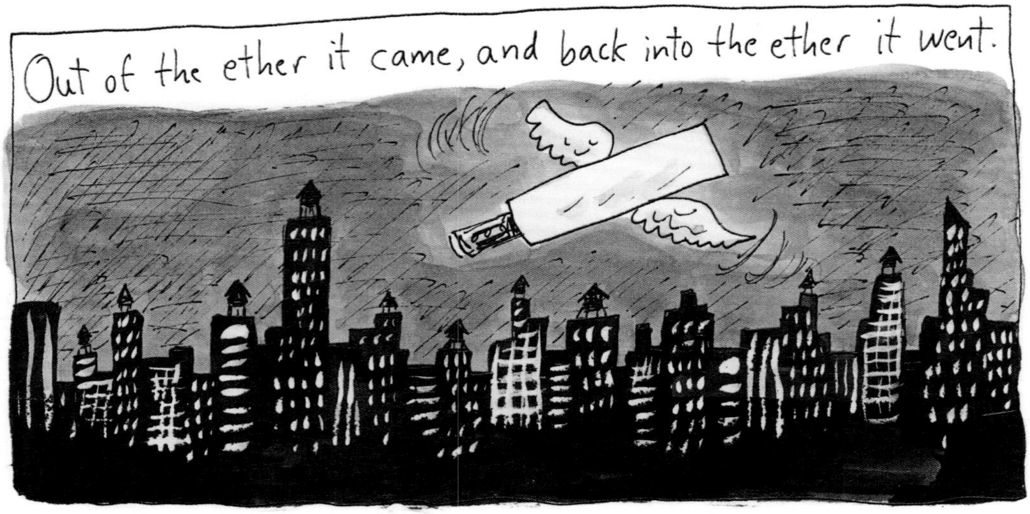
Out of the ether it came, and back into the ether it went.

Surprising things can happen at any time.

Sometimes when you're walking around, you decide you need to buy a lipstick at an off-brand yet oddly compelling store...

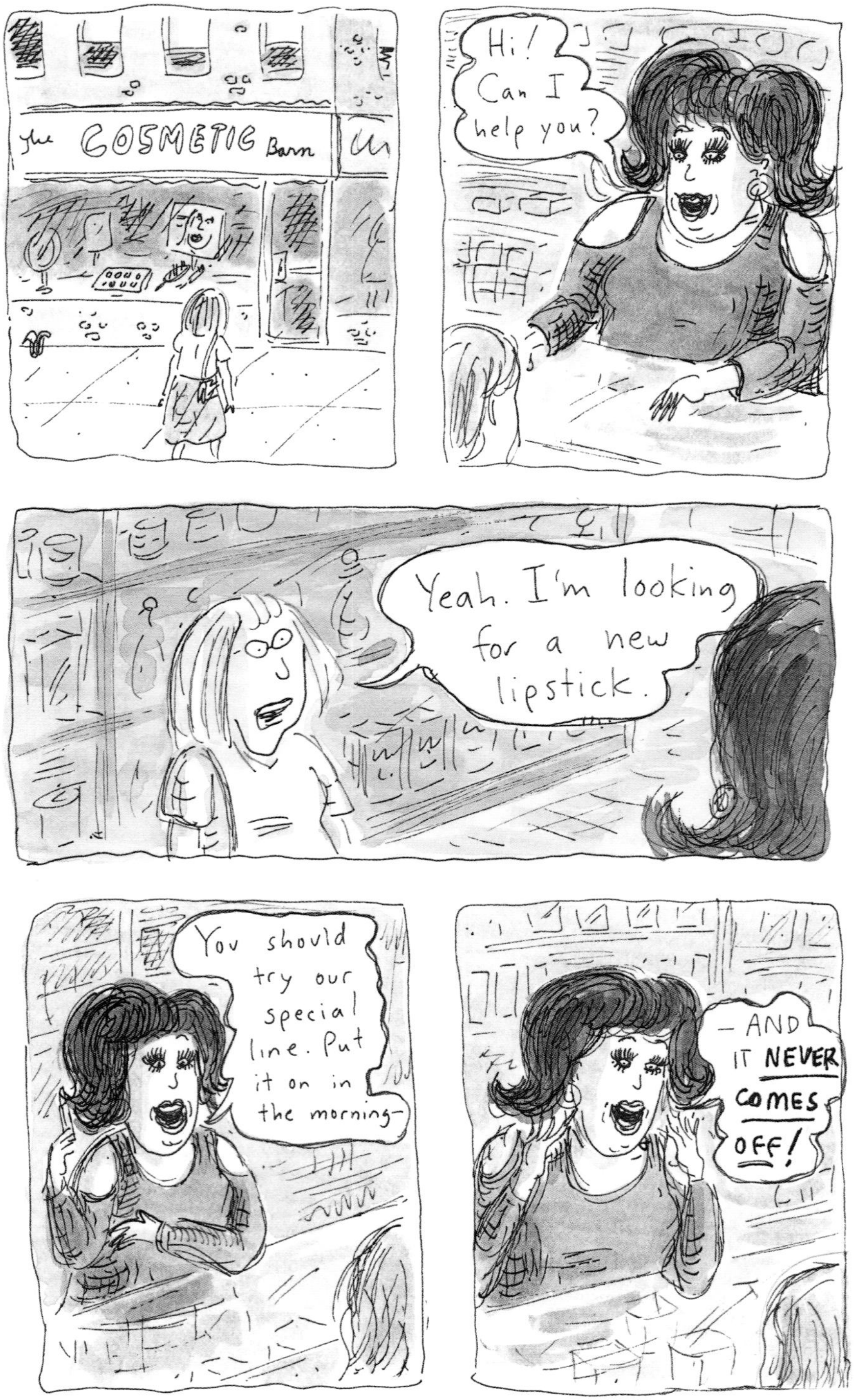
The COSMETIC Barn
Hi! Can I help you?
Yeah. I'm looking for a new lipstick.
You should try our special line. Put it on in the morning-
-AND IT NEVER COMES OFF!

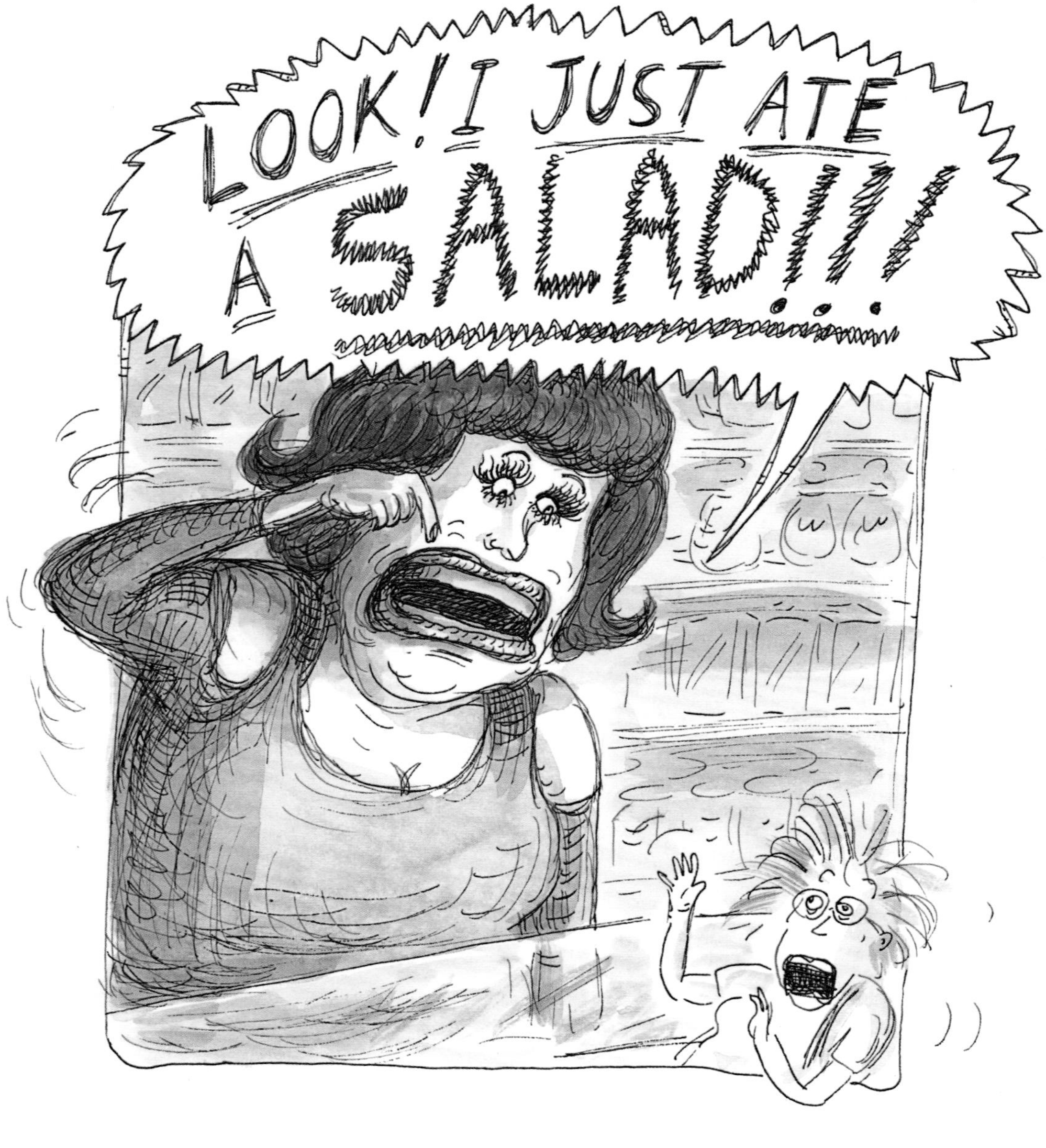
LOOK! I JUST ATE A SALAD!!!

While you're walking around,
keep your eyes open for interesting storefronts...

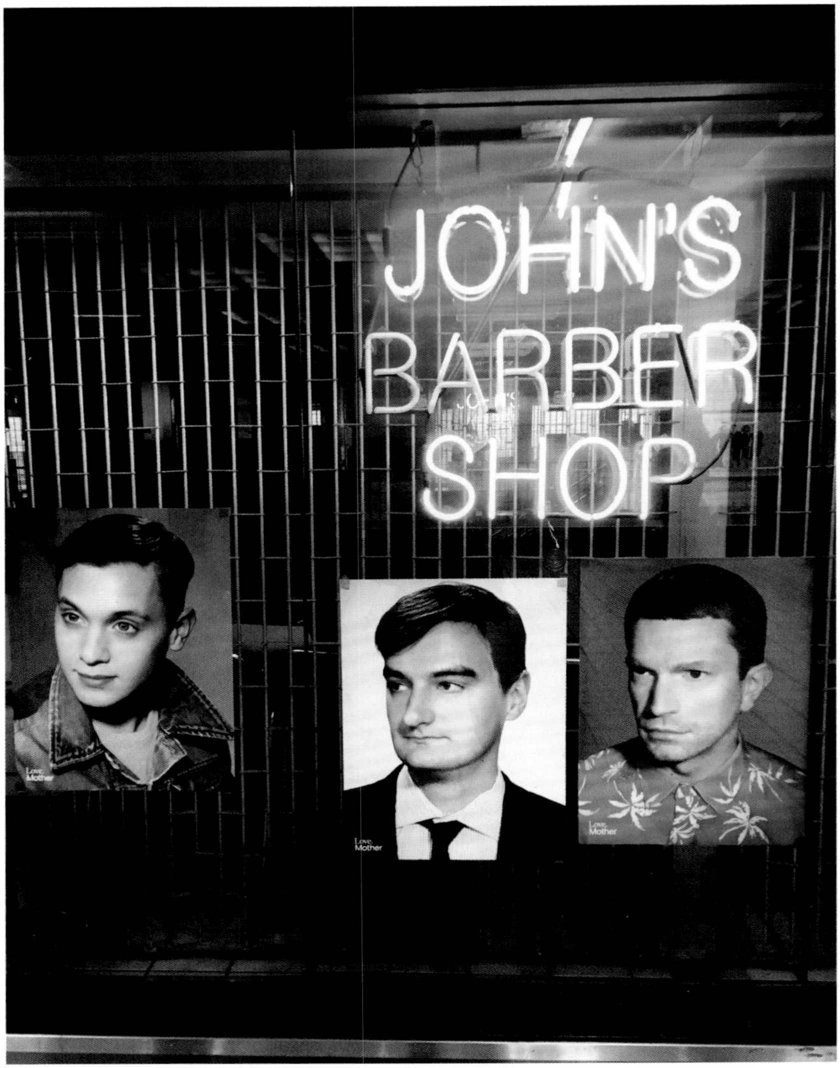
JOHN'S
BARBER
SHOP
Love
Mother
Love
Mother
Love
Mother

... or objects ...

An installation by Hërd Banister-Klein, perhaps?

... or doorways.

Maybe one day you will notice the amazing variety of standpipes.

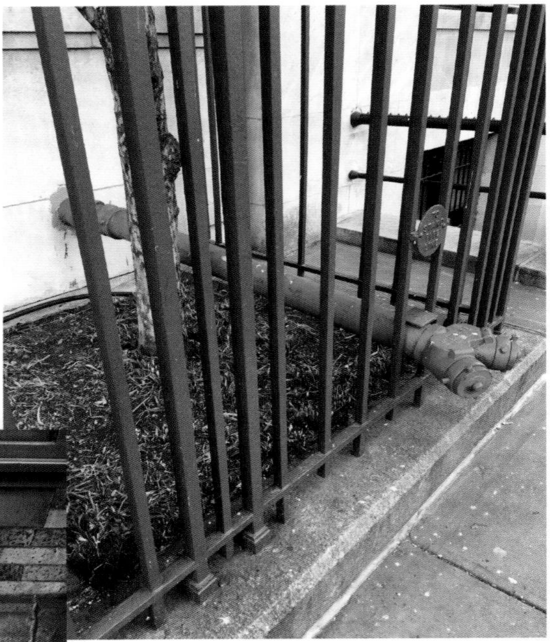

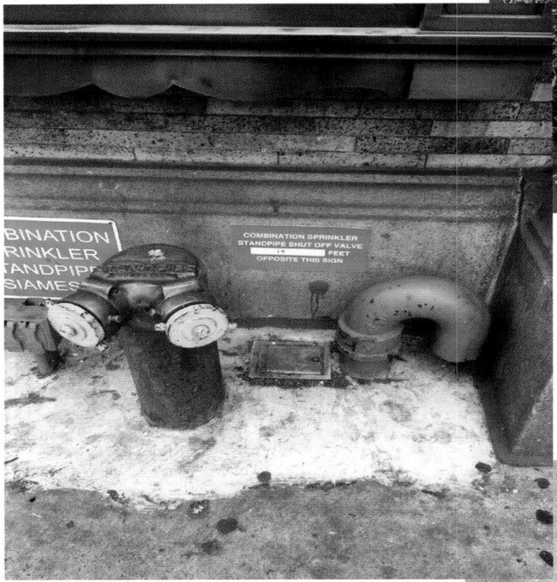
COMBINATION SPRINKLER
STANDPIPE SHUT OFF VALVE
FEET
OPPOSITE THIS SIGN

The more you notice them...

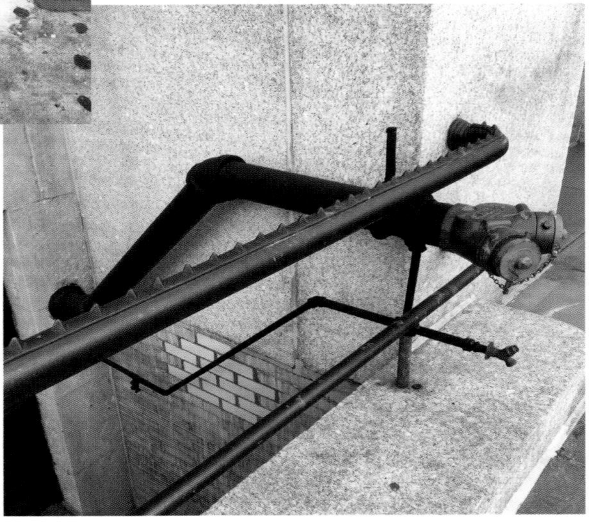

the more you will see.

This one goes by
the name of
"Trixxxi."

← ▭

And this one is —
obviously — The God of
All Standpipes. Don't
get too close, and don't
make him angry.

▭ →

PERHAPS YOU WILL NOTICE THE MANY...

STORES OF MYSTERY

Fred's Drugs

Surrounded by cut-rate drug-and-cosmetic emporiums that sell, let's say, a bottle of XYZ shampoo for 79¢. Same bottle at Fred's? $2.09!!! How does he do it?

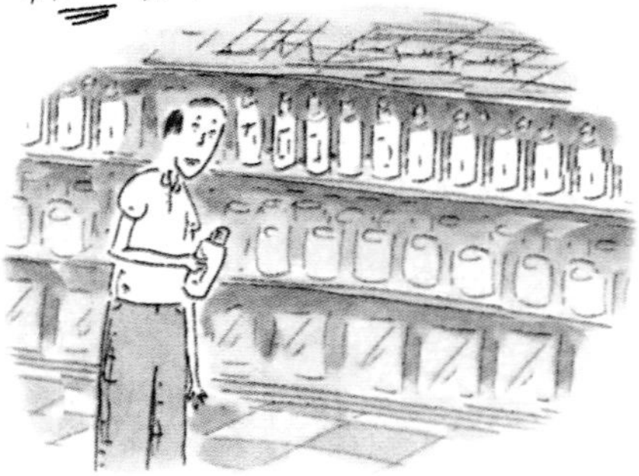

Beauty-Moi Frocks

Weird clothes, always five seasons out of date. Has been there forever. Store is usually pretty empty except for racks and racks of pantsuits and the like. Who shops here?

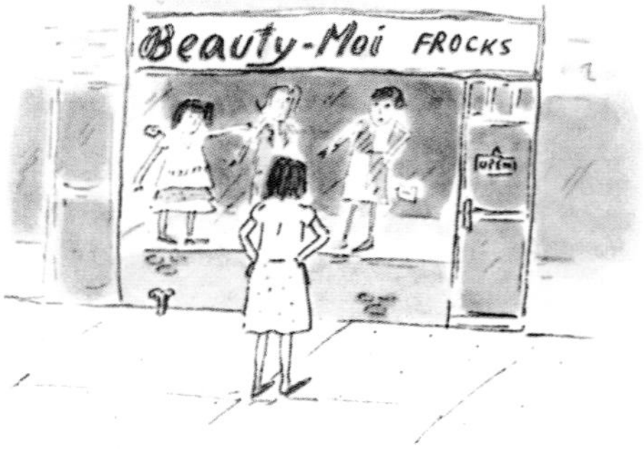
Beauty-Moi FROCKS

M & O Typewriter Supplies

This place has been closed whenever one has walked by it. However, it's *always* *there*, meaning somebody is continuing to pay rent on it. Why?

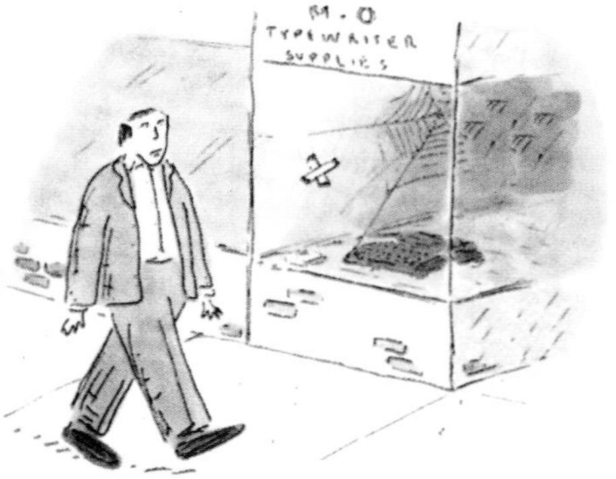
TYPEWRITER SUPPLIES

Tip-Top Goods

Boxes of saltines next to cartons of hair spray. Wigs, Christmas decorations, halter tops, institutional-sized jars of olives. Did all of this stuff "fall off a truck" or what?

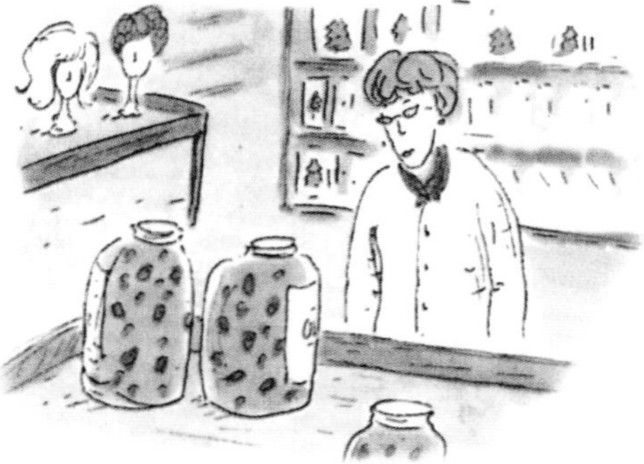

OR THE

ANCIENT LANDMARKS

OF NEW YORK CITY

Scaffold, West 81st Street
Is believed to have originated in the early 12th century A.D.

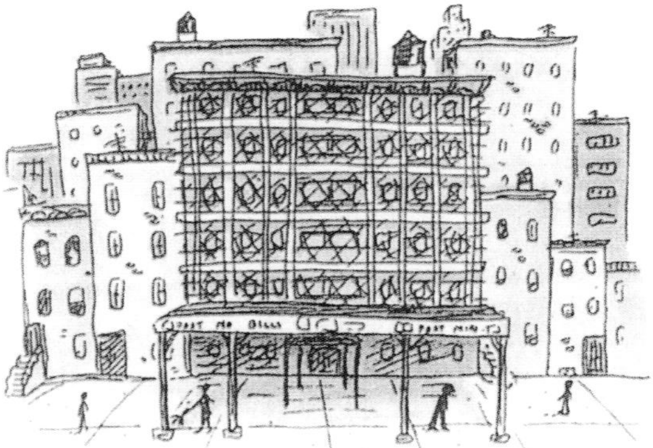
POST NO BILLS

Sidewalk Crater, Amsterdam Avenue
Has been there since the time of the Pharaohs.

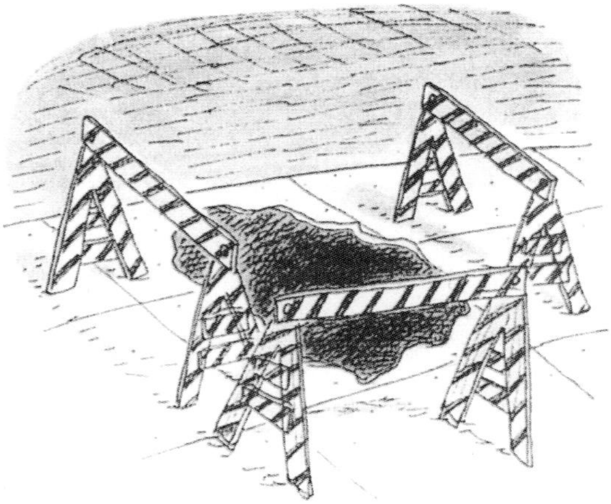

Half-Deconstructed Town House, East 19th Street
References to it have been found in the Old Testament.

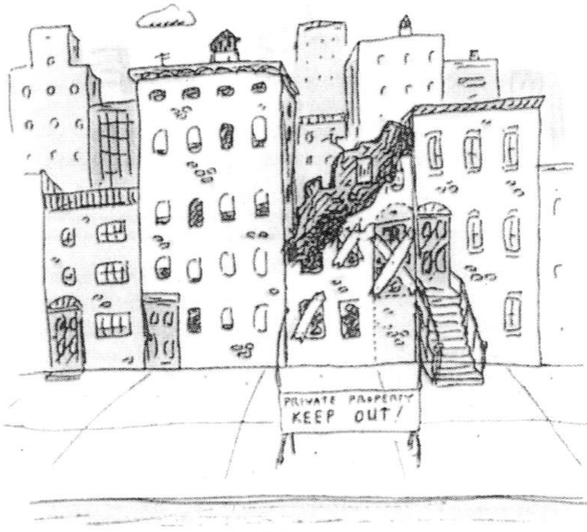
PRIVATE PROPERTY
KEEP OUT!

Abandoned Automobile, Riverside Drive
Fragments have been carbon-dated to the Jurassic period.

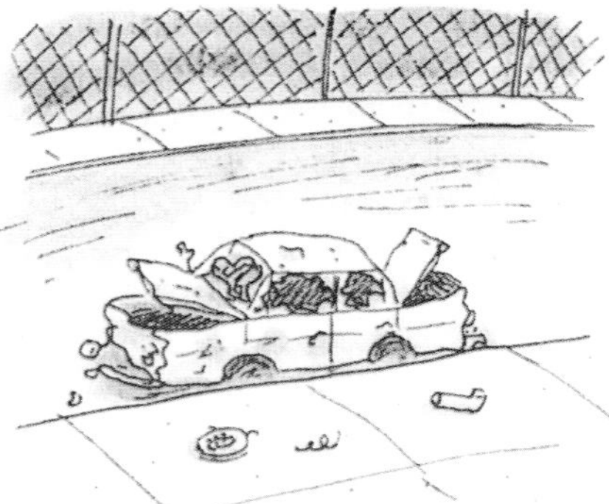

Walking is the best. But there are occasions when it's too far to walk or time is short. In that case, head for the nearest subway...

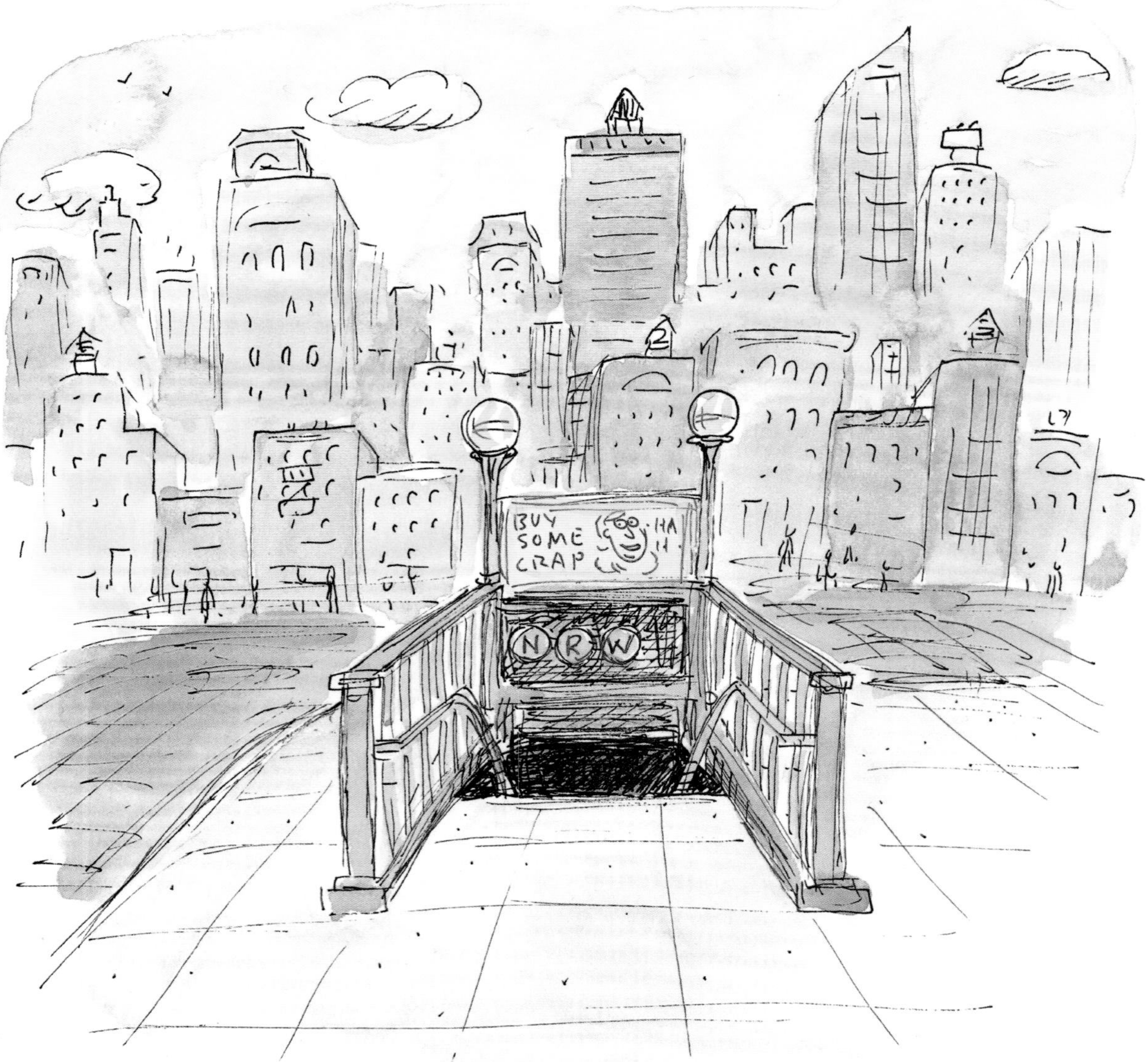
BUY
SOME
CRAP
HA
N
R
W

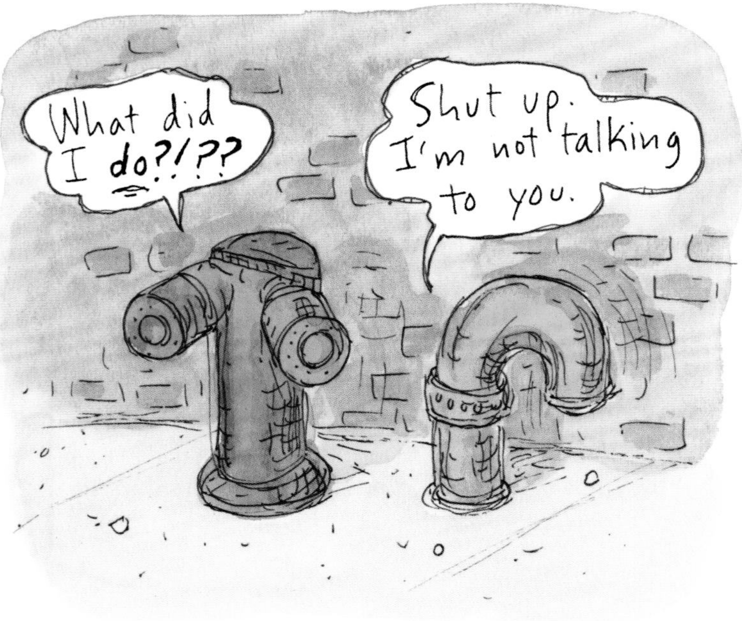
What did I do?!??
Shut up. I'm not talking to you.

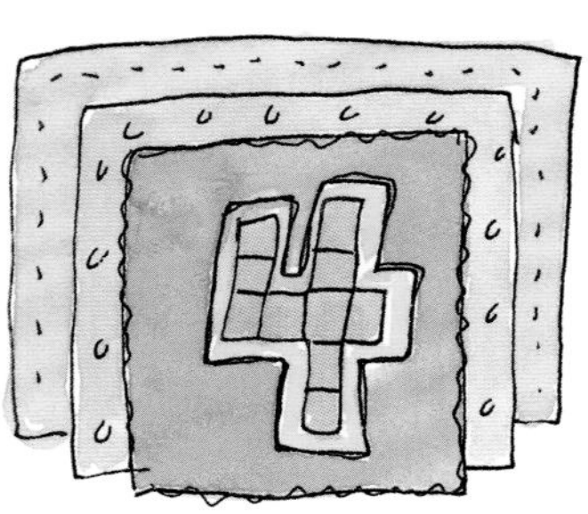
4

THE SUBWAY

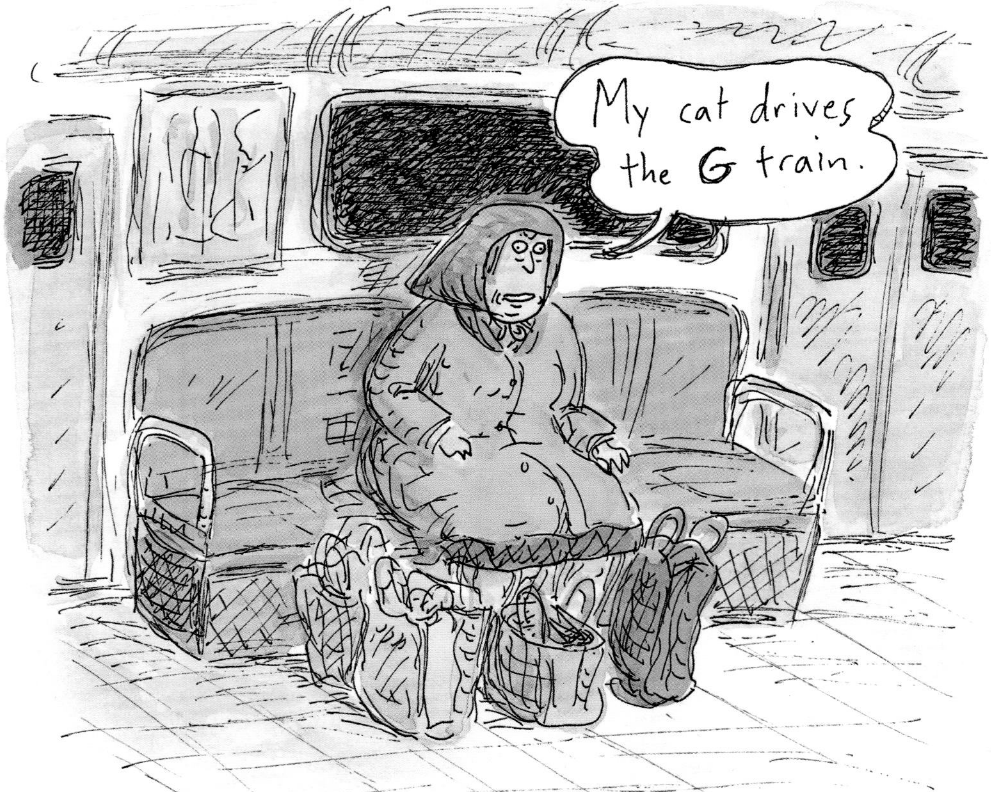
My cat drives the G train.

The sidewalk in New York is like a thin shell covering a vast honeycomb of pipes and tunnels. The ground under which you are walking has been almost completely excavated. It is best if you don't think about this...

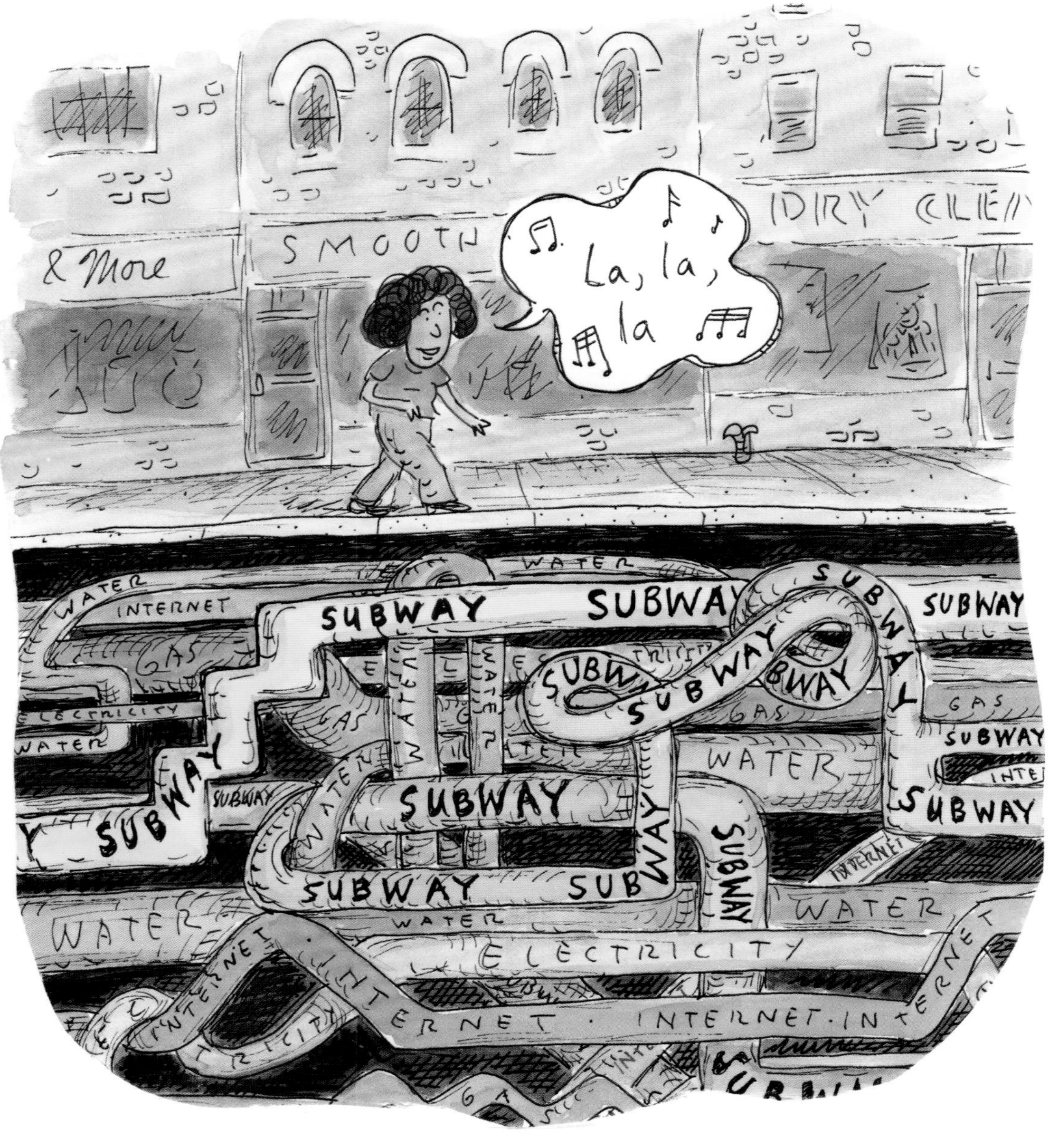
& More
SMOOTH
DRY CLE
La, la, la
WATER
INTERNET
SUBWAY
SUBWAY
SUBWAY
GAS
ELECTRICITY
WATER
SUBWAY
SUBWAY
WATER
SUBWAY
SUBWAY
SUBWAY
WATER
ELECTRICITY
INTERNET · INTERNET · INTERNET

When I was little, my parents and I occasionally took the subway from Newkirk Avenue in Brooklyn into Manhattan – what they called "going into town." These trips were for the sole purpose of seeing a play – almost always a musical, like Oklahoma or Man of La Mancha.

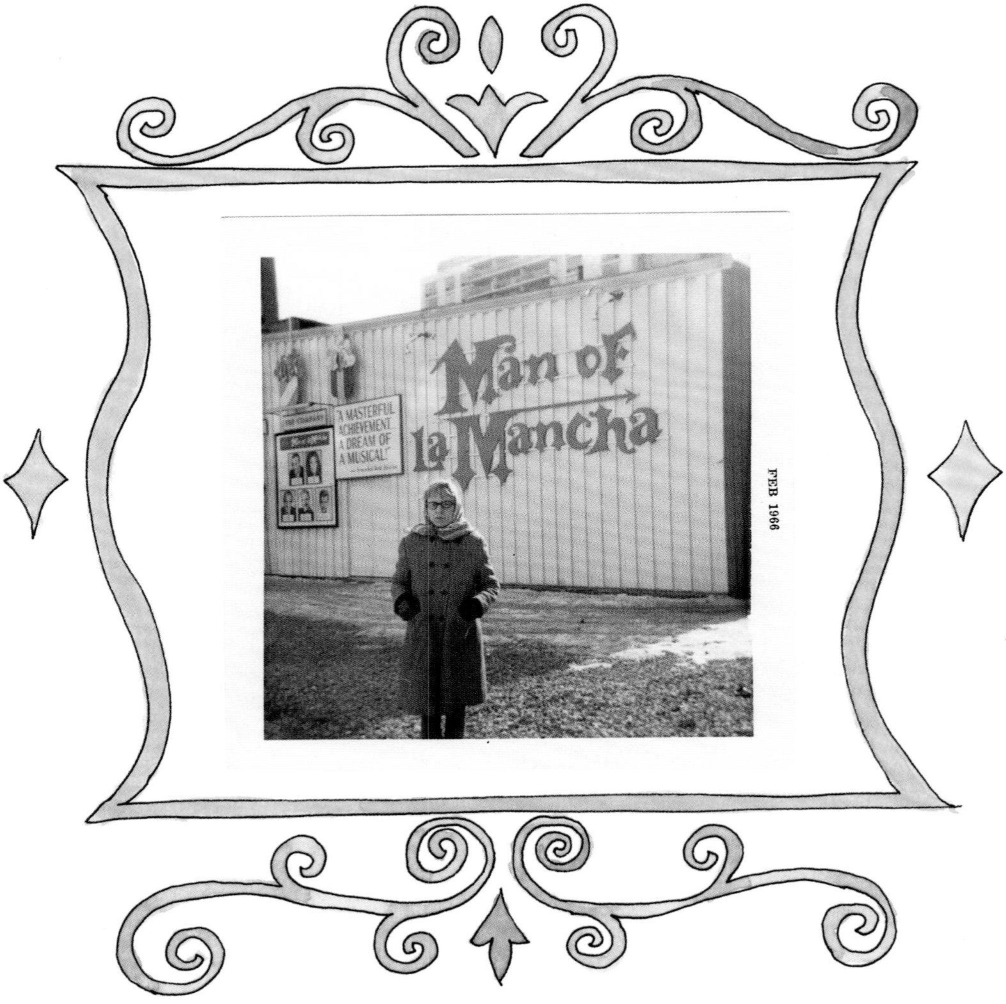

Man of
la Mancha
"A MASTERFUL
ACHIEVEMENT.
A DREAM OF
A MUSICAL!"
FEB 1966

We'd go in, see the play, get back on the subway, and go home. We did not walk around and explore, or eat - either before or after the play - at a restaurant near the theater. My mother blamed her "bad feet," but I suspect there were other concerns:

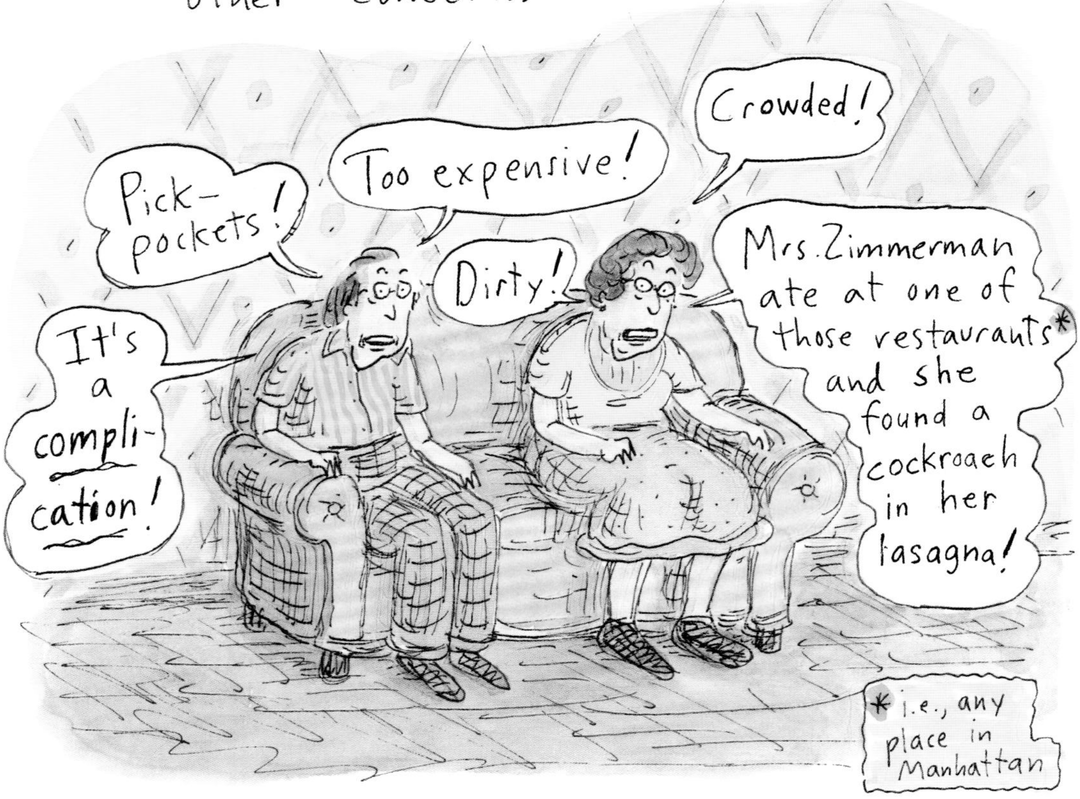
Pick-pockets!
Too expensive!
Crowded!
Dirty!
It's a complication!
Mrs. Zimmerman ate at one of those restaurants* and she found a cockroach in her lasagna!
* i.e., any place in Manhattan

There was only one restaurant they "trusted" to eat out in: a Chinese place one block from where we lived in Brooklyn.

Back in the day, one bought tokens to ride the subway.

One of my father's main pieces of advice to me was:

When you're going to the subway, ALWAYS HAVE A TOKEN IN YOUR HAND!

Because almost nothing is sadder than missing your train while you're fishing around for a token. He knew this.

Nowadays, of course, it's a Metrocard.

If you want to know New York, you have to learn the subway so get yourself one of these:

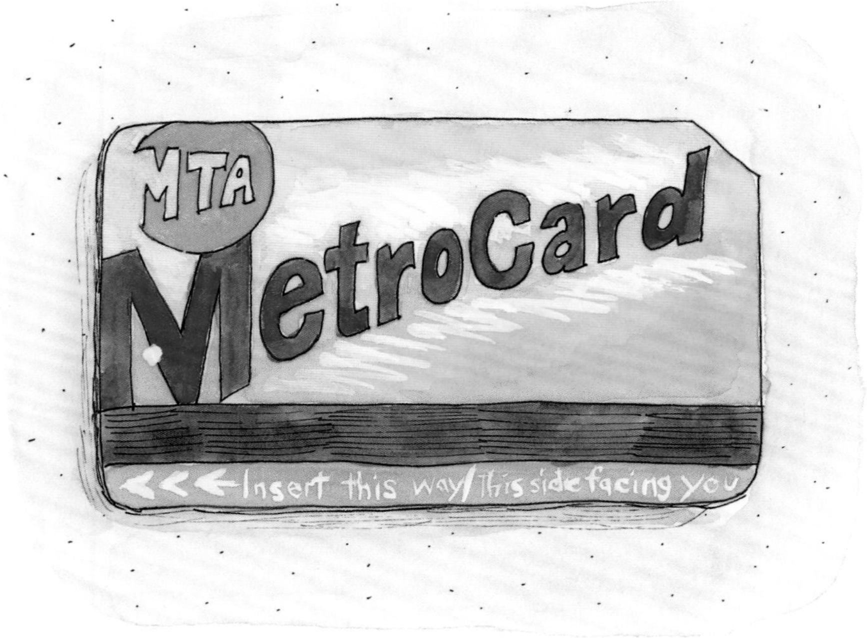
MTA
MetroCard
Insert this way/This side facing you

(It's helpful to know how the subway relates to the layout* of Manhattan.)

*See Chapter 2, Basic Layout

As I mentioned before, Manhattan has an **EAST** side and a **WEST** side.

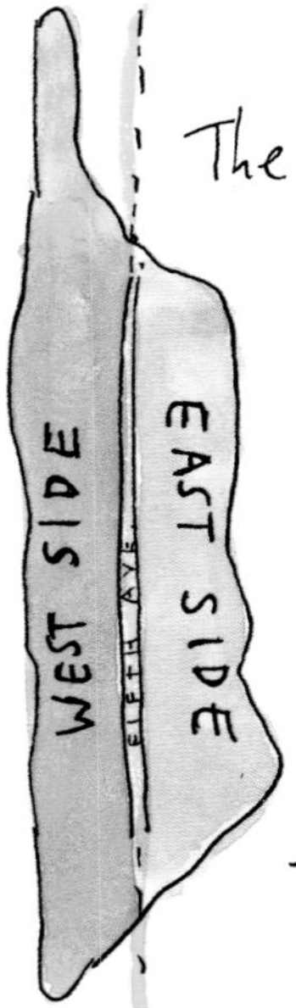
WEST SIDE
FIFTH AVE
EAST SIDE

The 1, 2, and 3 run—mostly—up SEVENTH AVE. & BROADWAY

The 2 & 3 are express.

The 1 is a local.

The 1 stops at every stop.

The 2 & 3 stop at the major cross-streets.

The 4, 5, and 6 run—mostly—up LEXINGTON AVE.

The 4 & 5 are express.

The 6 is a local.

The 6 stops at every stop.

The 4 & 5 stop at the major cross-streets.

The 1, 2, and 3 are your West Side trains.

The 4, 5, and 6 are your East Side trains.

The letter trains are more complicated. They go up and down the length of Manhattan and also across. They do weird jig-jags. And, like the number trains, most of them meander into the other boroughs.

Gradually, all of this will make sense, except late at night, or on weekends, or when there's construction, when the trains can get a little "devil-may-care."

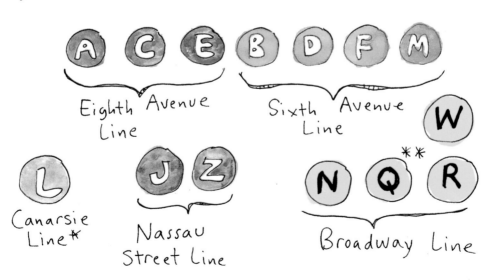

Eighth Avenue Line

Sixth Avenue Line

Canarsie Line *

Nassau Street Line

Broadway Line

(* Good for traversing 14th Street)

(** part of the new Second Av. subway line) (!!!!!)

An important train to know about is the SHUTTLE. The SHUTTLE goes on this route:

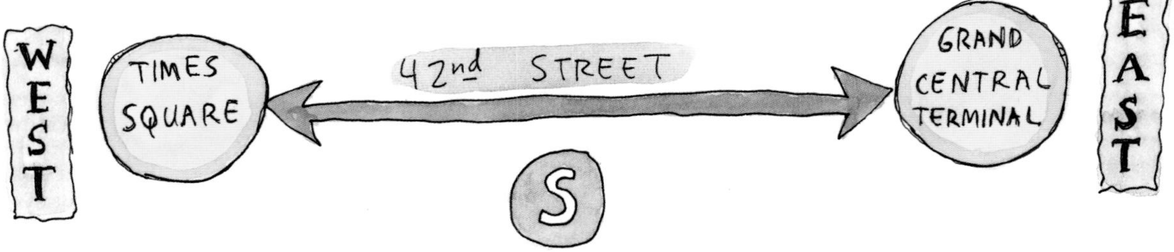
WEST
TIMES SQUARE
42nd STREET
GRAND CENTRAL TERMINAL
EAST
S

These two stations are very important because so many subway lines pass through them, which means that at those stations, you can transfer from one line to another - i.e., switch to another line without paying an additional fare.

HOW DOES THIS WORK?

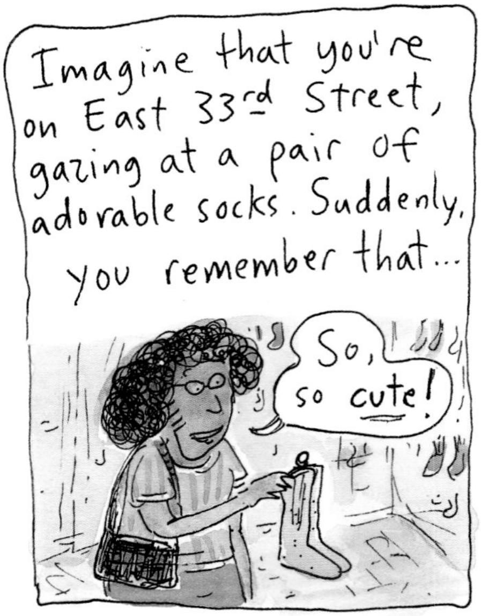
Imagine that you're on East 33rd Street, gazing at a pair of adorable socks. Suddenly, you remember that...
So, so cute!

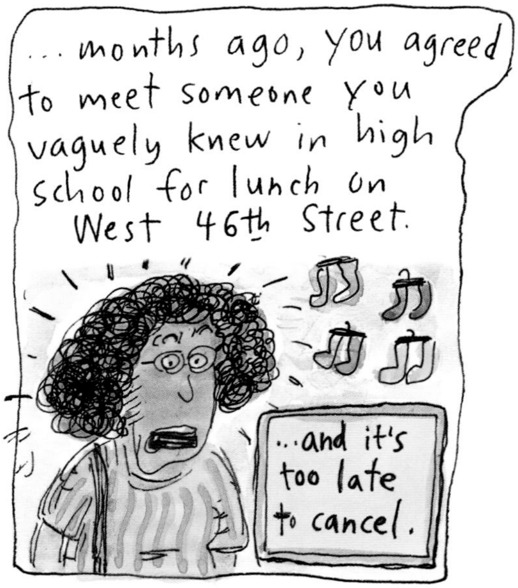
...months ago, you agreed to meet someone you vaguely knew in high school for lunch on West 46th Street.
...and it's too late to cancel.

It's also too late to walk. So you go to the nearest subway - in this case, the one on Park Ave. South and 33rd.

Get on the **UPTOWN** ⑥ and get off at Grand Central.

Take the SHUTTLE to Times Square - 42nd Street.

Exit the station and run four blocks uptown like a bat out of hell to that godforsaken restaurant which is on, like, Tenth Avenue or some such, because now you're _REALLY_ late.

"BON APPETIT!"

OUTTA MY WAY

The best thing to do is download a subway map onto your phone. In between cat videos, Instagram, learning Sanskrit, and bouts of Carton Crush®, you can study it.

And one last thing:

If the train is very crowded, and you see an empty car, don't think:

or
I must be some kind of genius!
Wow! I'm in LUCK!! Plenty o' seats for ME!!!

An empty car in the middle of a bunch of packed cars means that the air conditioning or heating is on the fritz; a nut is holding court; someone has had a pungent accident; or there's a dead person in there.

P.S.: TAXIS

Every so often, when one has procrastinated oneself into a corner, or one finds oneself in a remote area far from a subway line like Twelfth Avenue, or when one is schlepping something, or when one is simply exhausted and cannot take another step, one might want to hail a yellow cab. Here's some stuff you'll need to know:

> If the roof light (that thing with the numbers and letters) is **LIT**, the cab is empty.

> If the roof light is **NOT** **LIT**, that means that the taxi is occupied or the driver is off duty.

A.   B.

HOW TO HAIL A CAB

Step off curb facing traffic.

Raise arm*
Some people yell "TAXI!!!" or whistle. I do not.

Cab will pull over. Open the back door and get in. The end.

*Make sure you're not stealing someone else's cab. This is very bad form unless you are dying. It's also bad taxi karma. Cabs take cash or credit cards.

(Some people prefer to use Uber, Lyft, etc. I prefer the good old yellow cab, unless there are no cabs to be had. Maybe it's because of the instant-gratification factor. You need a cab, you hail a cab, you're in a cab.)

P. P. S. Don't neglect buses. These lumbering, oblong lane-hogs are slow as "molasses in January," and don't come for a long time, only to arrive in bunches. But sometimes, when you're not in a rush, they are a fun way to travel and see the sights above ground: the people, the stores, the mish-mosh of architectural styles. Try to get a window seat.

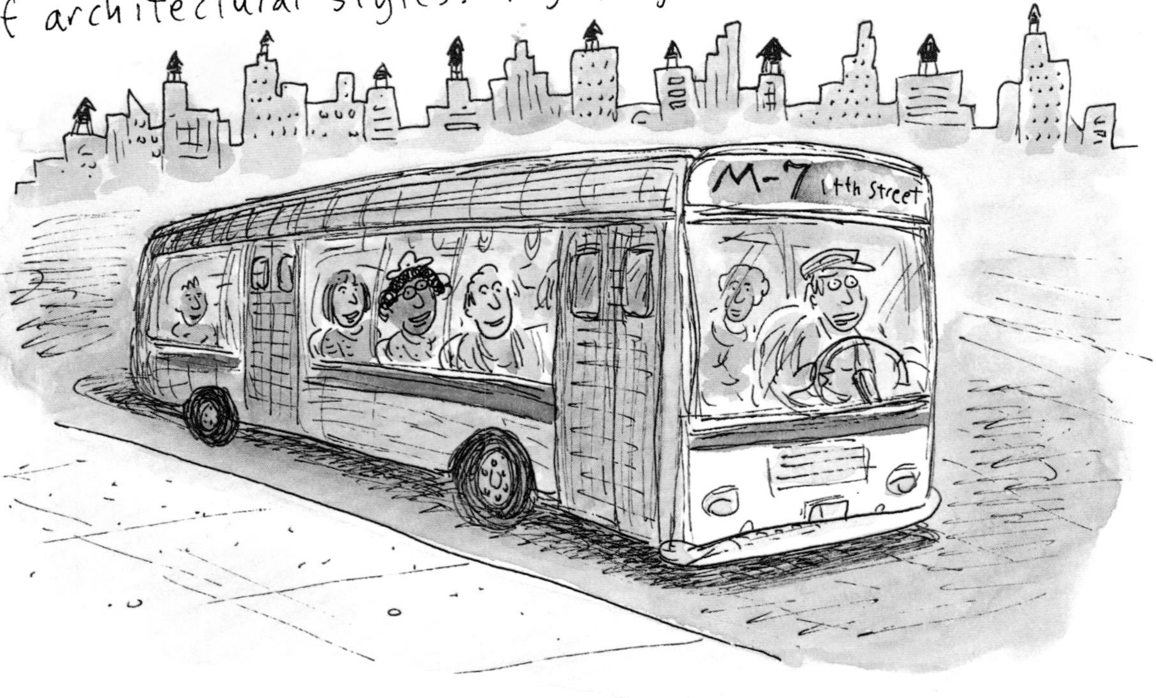
M-7
14th Street

[Make sure you board the one that starts with "M" or you'll wind up in Queens or the Bronx or some other place that's not in Manhattan.]

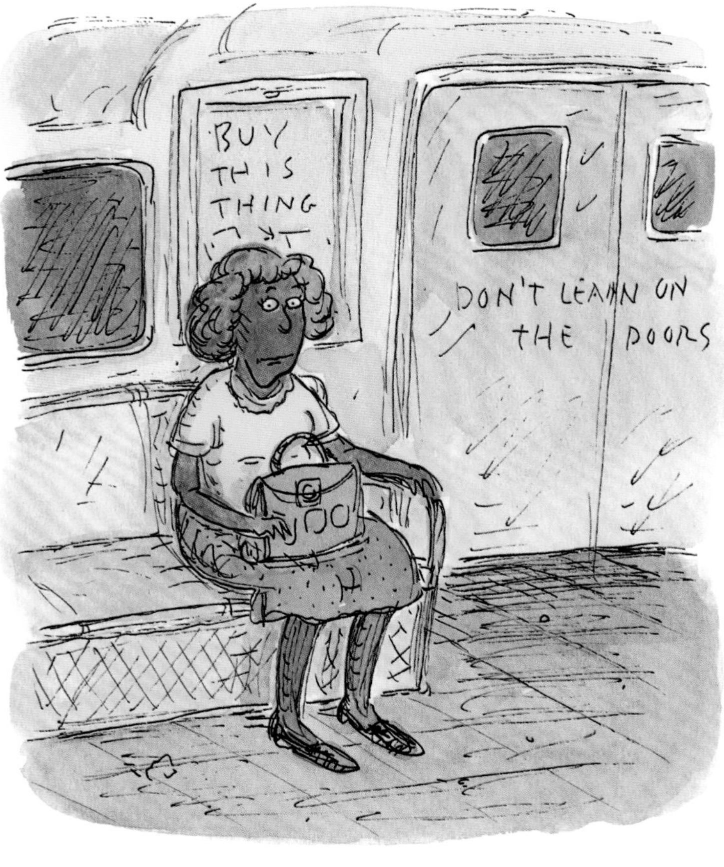
BUY
THIS
THING
DON'T LEAN ON
THE DOORS

STUFF TO DO

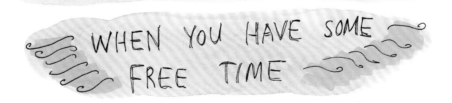

WHEN YOU HAVE SOME FREE TIME

(AND HOPEFULLY, YOU HAVE A LITTLE)

One of the many things I love about Manhattan is that you never really have to face that existential dilemma you might have to face if you lived in, say, rural Nebraska:

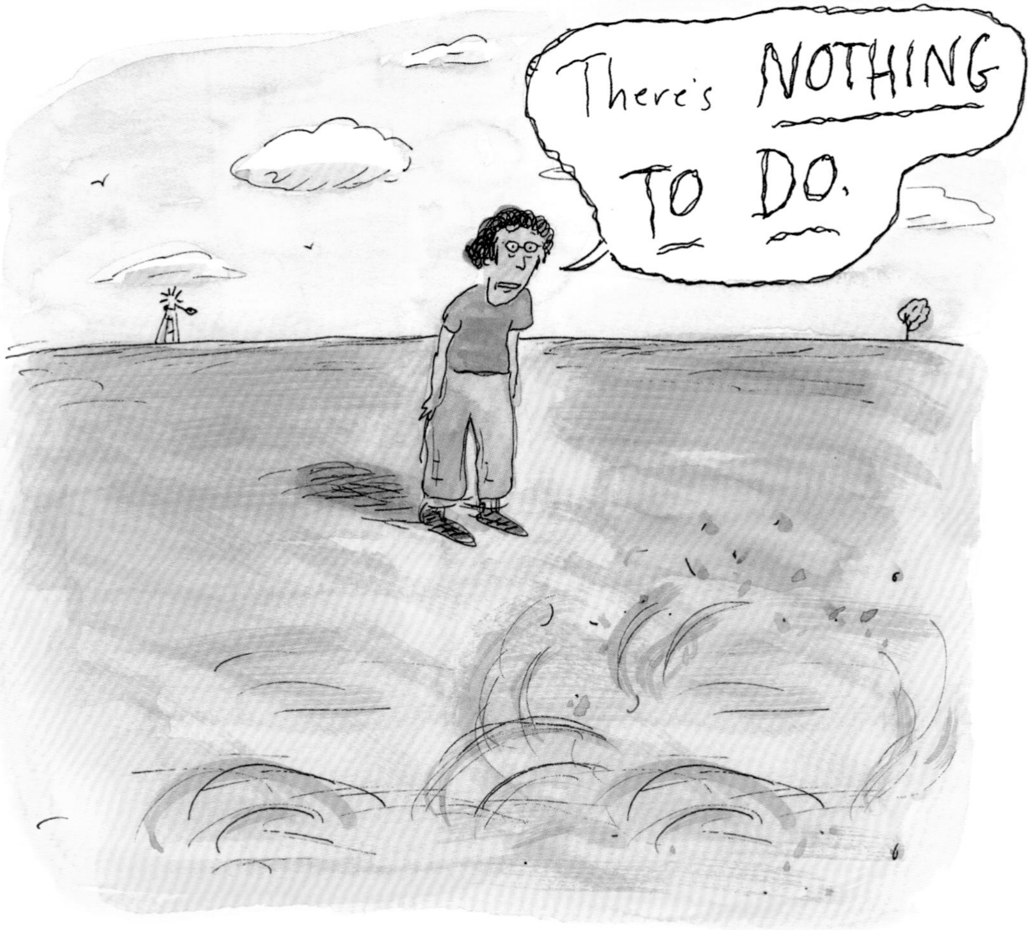
There's NOTHING TO DO.

If you feel that there's "nothing to do" while you're in Manhattan, then this is **DEFINITELY** not the book you should be reading. Also, you might be dead.

Day or night, any day of the week, any time of the year, including the dreaded wasteland of Christmas Day, you can find stuff to do. And it doesn't all cost big bucks.

'Bye!

Museums and galleries are great places, if you like to look at stuff that other people made, and not all of them charge admission. The Met, for example, is a "pay what you want" museum.

HERE IS A PARTIAL LIST OF ART MUSEUMS:

- METROPOLITAN MUSEUM OF ART ("THE MET")
- MUSEUM OF MODERN ART ("MOMA")
- THE WHITNEY
- THE GUGGENHEIM
- THE FRICK
- THE RUBIN MUSEUM

- THE NEW MUSEUM
- THE AMERICAN FOLK ART MUSEUM
- MUSEUM OF THE CITY OF NEW YORK
- THE MORGAN LIBRARY AND MUSEUM
- THE JEWISH MUSEUM
- THE COOPER-HEWITT

The Met's permanent collection contains over two million "things": paintings and sculptures and costumes and snuff boxes and ceramic tiles and armor and all kinds of stuff from all over the world and from every era. If you are feeling low, it's possible that looking at a french tassel from the 18th century might cheer you up.

The great thing about the Met is that you can never see all of it. There is just too much. No matter how many times you go, you will always discover something great you've never seen before. And this doesn't even take into account the new exhibits that are always being mounted! In that way, the Met is like a microcosm of New York itself. There is a sense of the infinite. And you know that by the time you've seen everything (which is impossible, anyway) some of the old stuff will have vanished, and there will be new things to see.

You can immerse yourself in

Armorland!

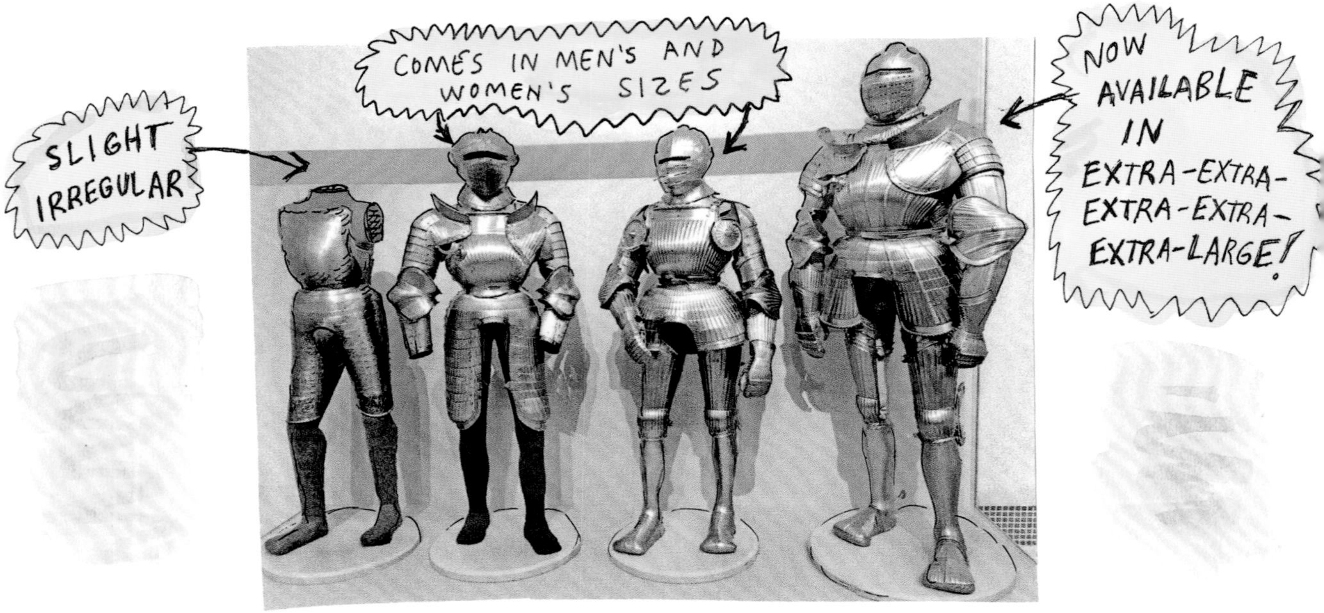

SLIGHT IRREGULAR
COMES IN MEN'S AND WOMEN'S SIZES
NOW AVAILABLE IN EXTRA-EXTRA-EXTRA-EXTRA-EXTRA-LARGE!

The Met has armor from all over the world, not just the clanky metal kind. There's armor from Japan, China, the Philippines, Tibet, Turkey, Iran, and more.

Or you can look at old paintings and invent stories for them:

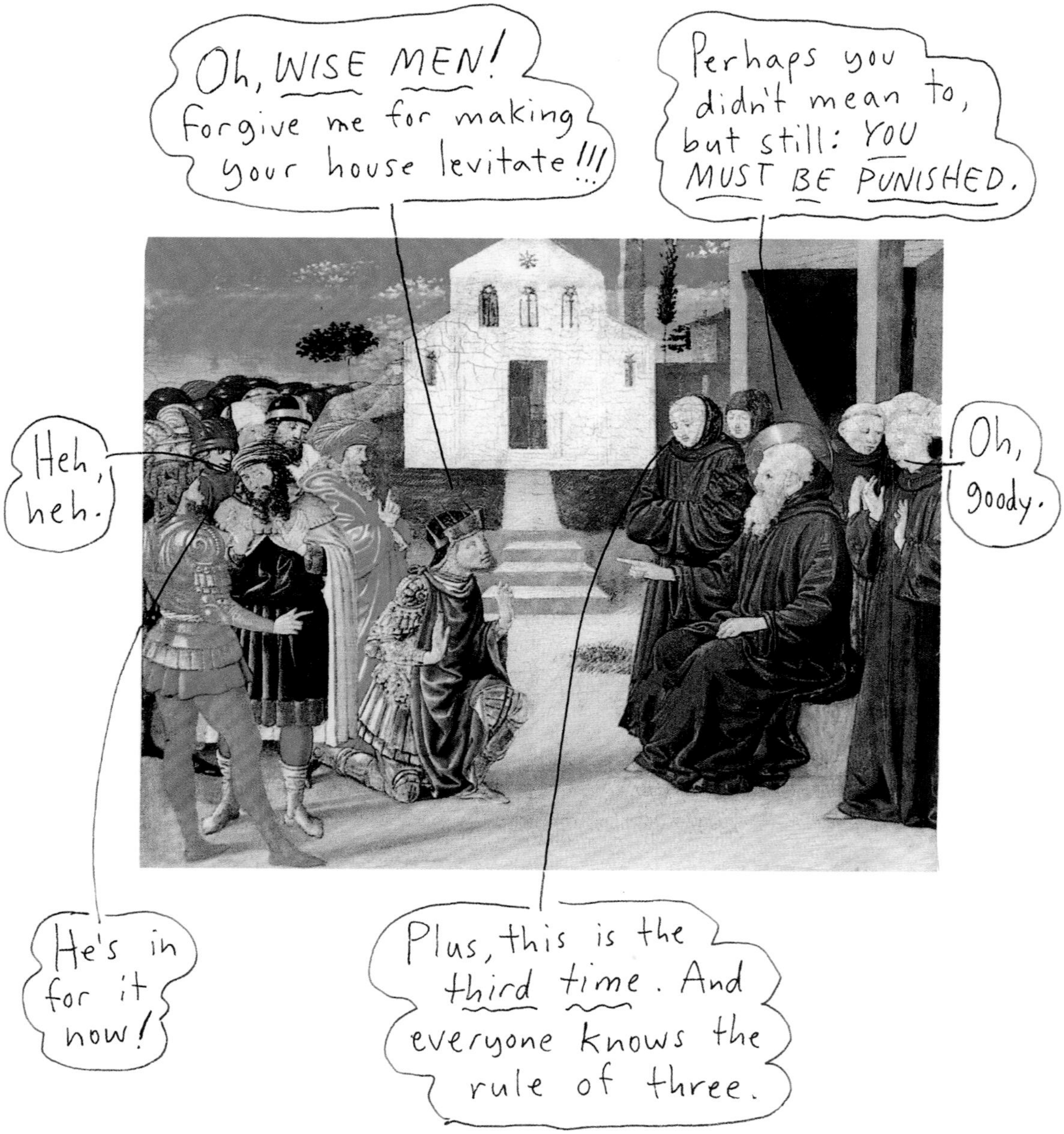

Oh, WISE MEN! Forgive me for making your house levitate!!!
Perhaps you didn't mean to, but still: YOU MUST BE PUNISHED.
Heh, heh.
Oh, goody.
He's in for it now!
Plus, this is the third time. And everyone knows the rule of three.

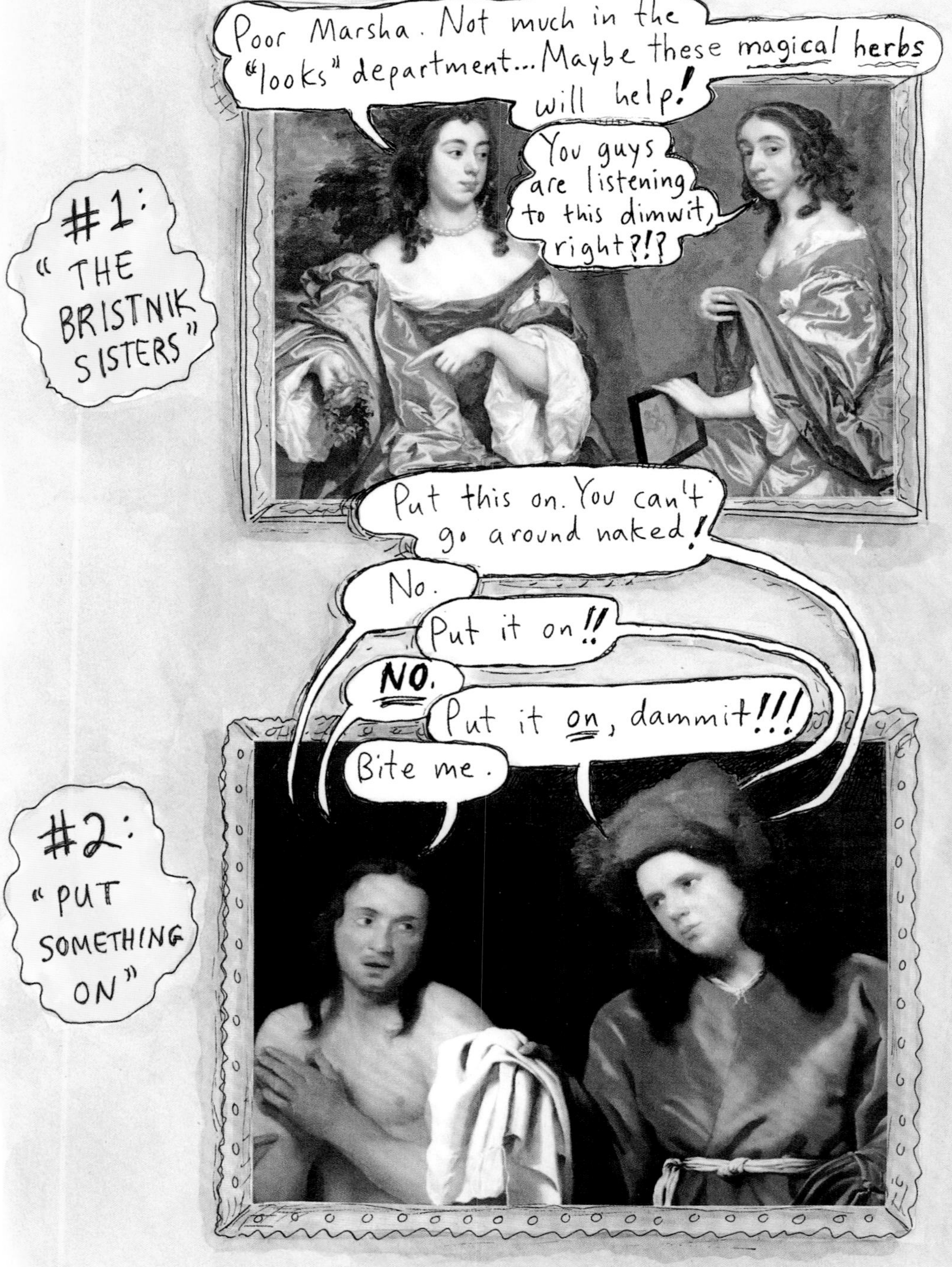
#1: "THE BRISTNIK SISTERS"
Poor Marsha. Not much in the "looks" department... Maybe these magical herbs will help!
You guys are listening to this dimwit, right?!?
#2: "PUT SOMETHING ON"
Put this on. You can't go around naked!
No.
Put it on!!
NO.
Put it on, dammit!!!
Bite me.

Or, get fashion tips!

Next time you get your hair cut, ask for a "Zazzera" - the "in" style in late 15th-century Venice.

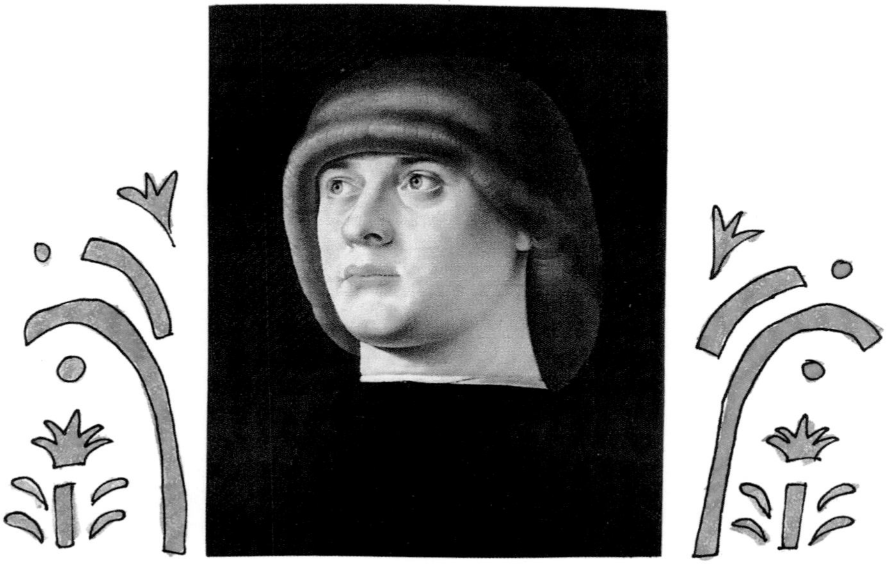

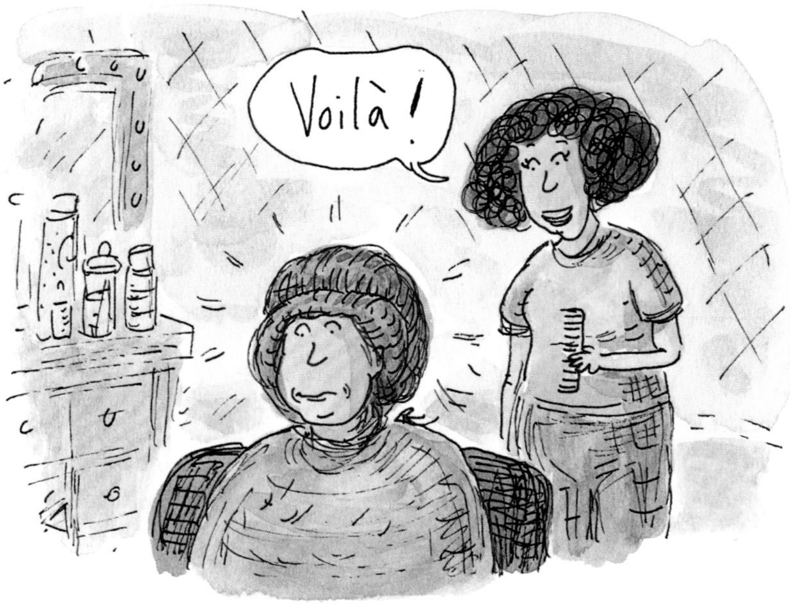
Voilà!

But maybe the best thing about the Met is that even at the height of the tourist season – what some people call "the holidays" – when Manhattan can seem just a tad too crowded, you can always find a place to be...

ALONE.

Another amazing museum is the American Museum of Natural History on Central Park West and 79th Street. There are over 33 million specimens here - plants, animals, fossils, gems, skeletons, and lots more.

My favorite item on exhibit is the 34-ton meteorite called Ahnighito.

It is <u>SO HEAVY</u> that it rests on supports that go straight through the museum <u>ALL THE WAY DOWN TO THE BEDROCK OF MANHATTAN</u>.

It is 4.5 billion years old - almost as old as the Sun. Respect must be paid.

And remember: if you get museum'd out, it's not a class trip. You can leave whenever you want. There's lots of other stuff to do.

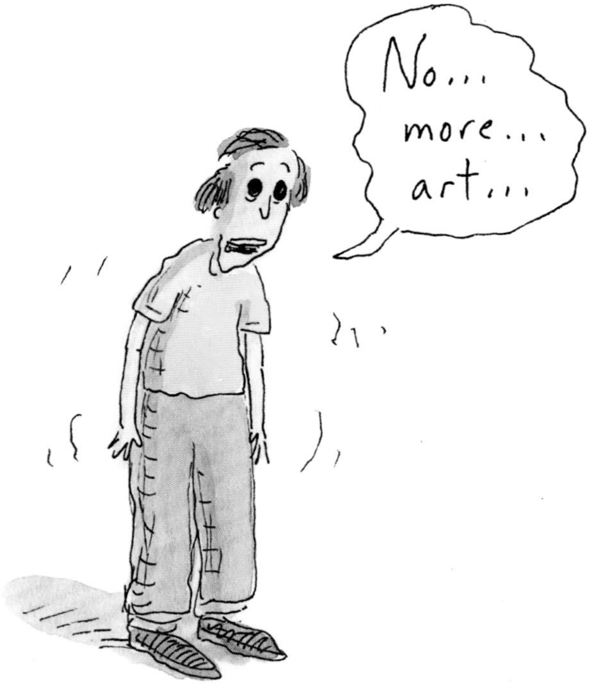
No...
more...
art...

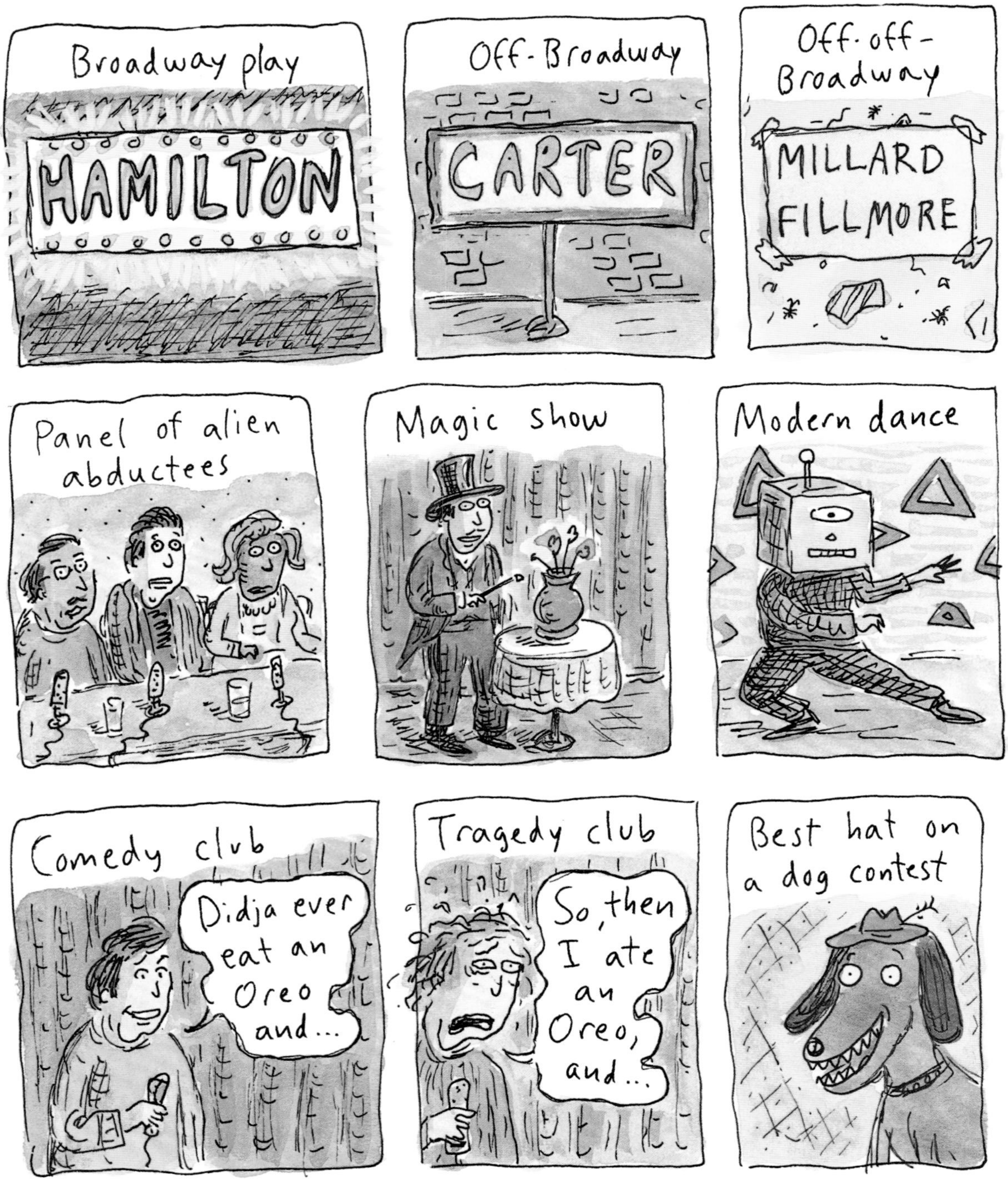
Broadway play
HAMILTON
Off-Broadway
CARTER
Off-off-Broadway
MILLARD FILLMORE
Panel of alien abductees
Magic show
Modern dance
Comedy club
Didja ever eat an Oreo and...
Tragedy club
So, then I ate an Oreo, and...
Best hat on a dog contest

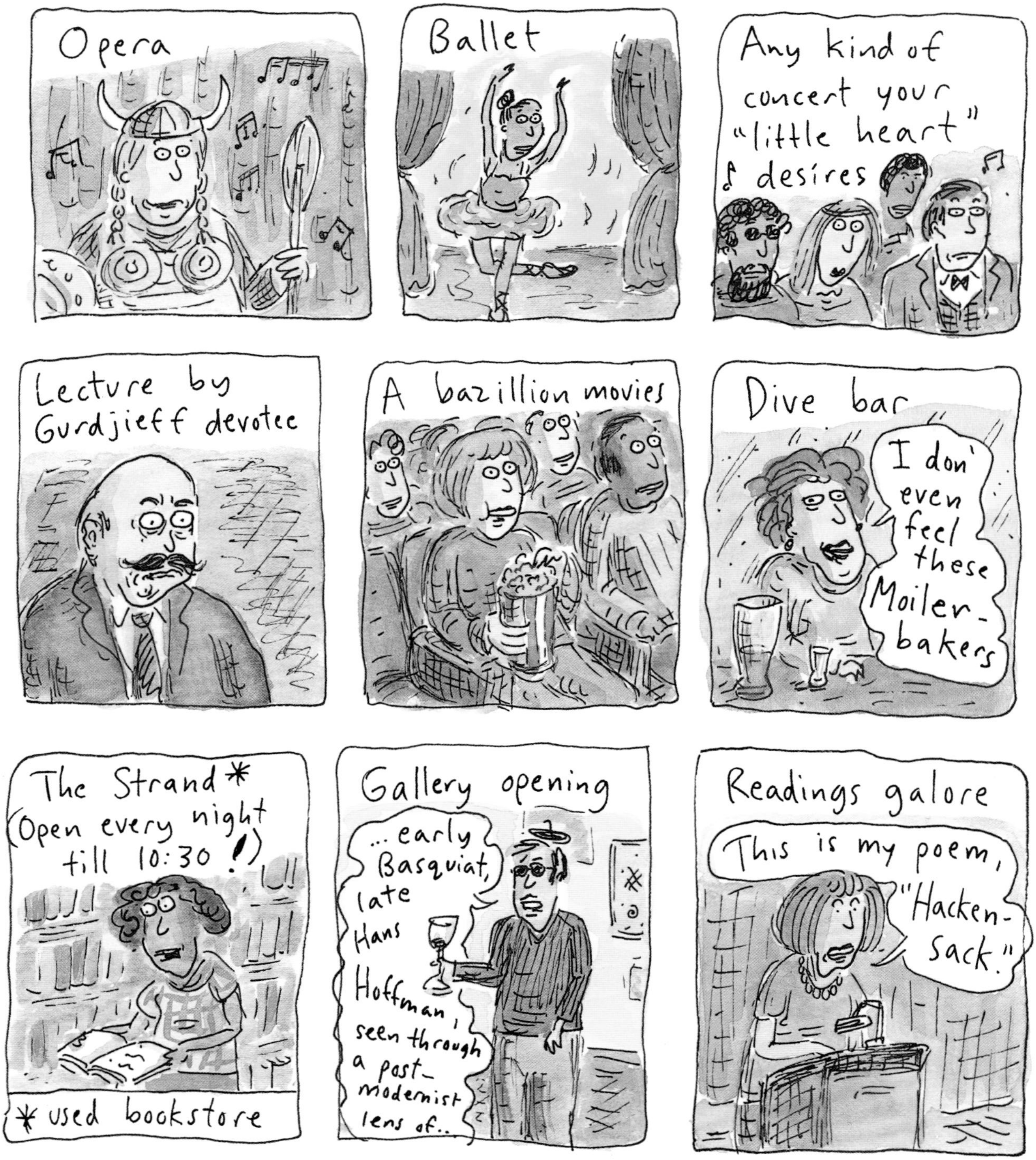

Opera
Ballet
Any kind of concert your "little heart" desires
Lecture by Gurdjieff devotee
A bazillion movies
Dive bar
I don' even feel these Moiler-bakers
The Strand* (Open every night till 10:30!)
* used bookstore
Gallery opening
...early Basquiat, late Hans Hoffman, seen through a post-modernist lens of..
Readings galore
This is my poem, "Hacken-Sack."

And, of course, there's always shopping. Not necessarily buying. Just... SHOPPING:

Hmmm...
MAJILLIONAIRES' WIVES DRESS HUT
May I help you?
I'd like to try something on.
Dressing room's this way.
Nah... I don't think it's "me."

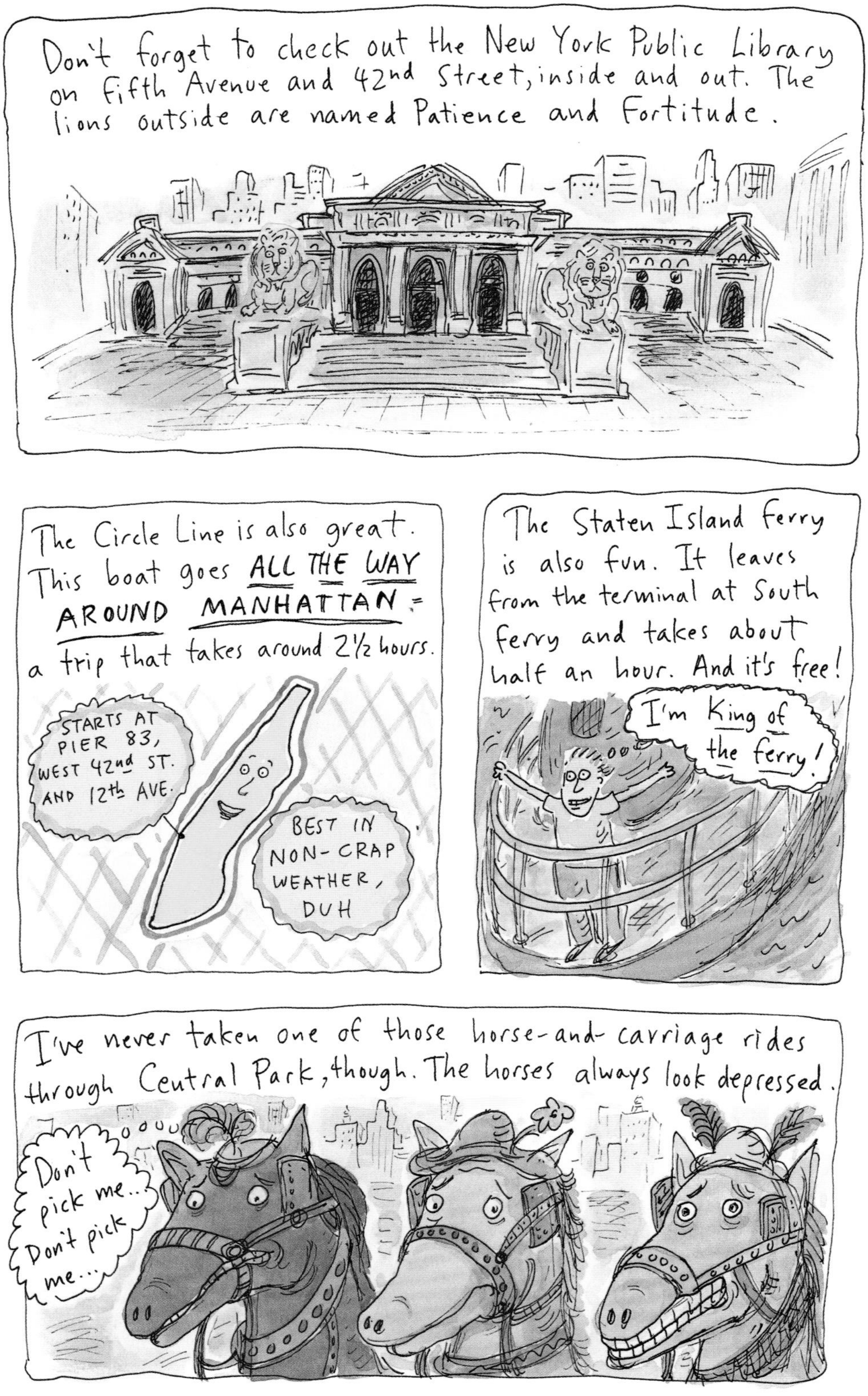
Don't forget to check out the New York Public Library on Fifth Avenue and 42nd Street, inside and out. The lions outside are named Patience and Fortitude.
The Circle Line is also great. This boat goes ALL THE WAY AROUND MANHATTAN = a trip that takes around 2½ hours.
STARTS AT PIER 83, WEST 42nd ST. AND 12th AVE.
BEST IN NON-CRAP WEATHER, DUH
The Staten Island ferry is also fun. It leaves from the terminal at South Ferry and takes about half an hour. And it's free!
I'm King of the ferry!
I've never taken one of those horse-and-carriage rides through Central Park, though. The horses always look depressed.
Don't pick me... Don't pick me...

One more suggestion: visit Grand Central Terminal, on East 42nd Street and Park Avenue. It was built at the turn of the last century and almost demolished in a fit of "everything old is bad and everything new is great" in the mid-1960s.

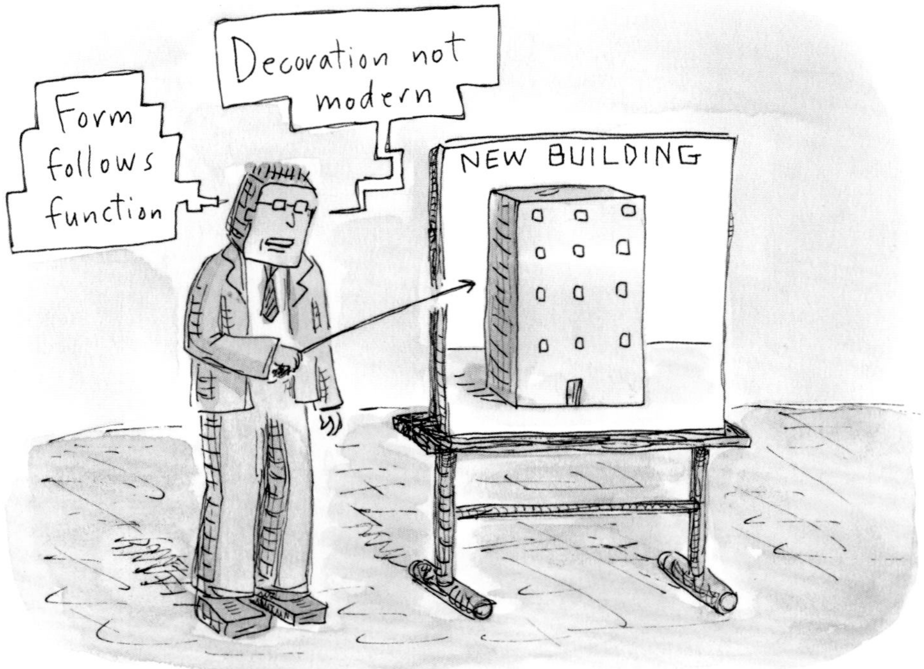
Form follows function
Decoration not modern
NEW BUILDING

This disaster was narrowly averted, thanks to the efforts of many far-sighted, influential New Yorkers, perhaps most notably Jacqueline Onassis, and in 1976, it was declared a National Historic Landmark.

Throughout most of my childhood and early adulthood - the 1970's and 1980s - GCT was a real skeevefest. Ugly billboards covered much of the original architecture, the restrooms were gross, and decades of grime had completely obscured the zodiac mural on the ceiling. But in the 1990s and 2000s, when the city had some money in its pockets again, it was renovated and restored to its original, breathtakingly lovely self. It's the first place I see when I come back to the city from Suburbia, and my favorite building in the city, for that reason - and also because it's a reminder that sometimes, the good guys win.

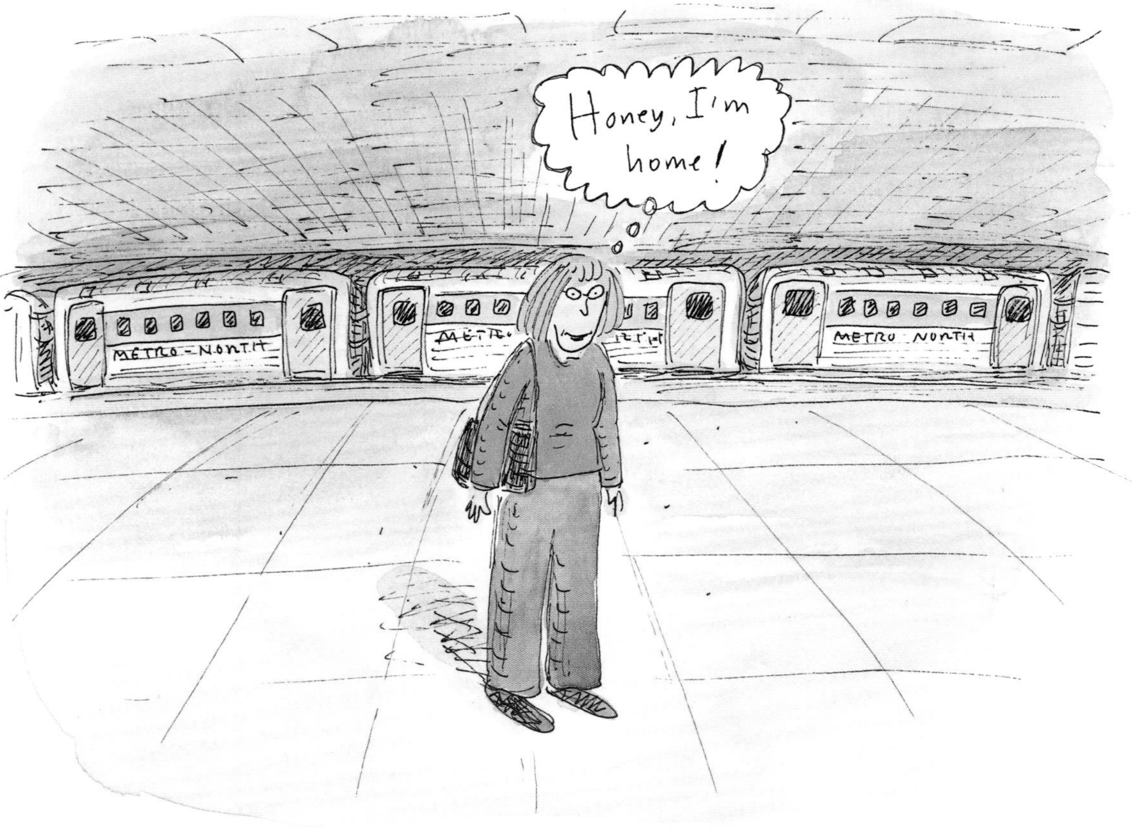
Honey, I'm home!
METRO-NORTH
METRO
METRO NORTH

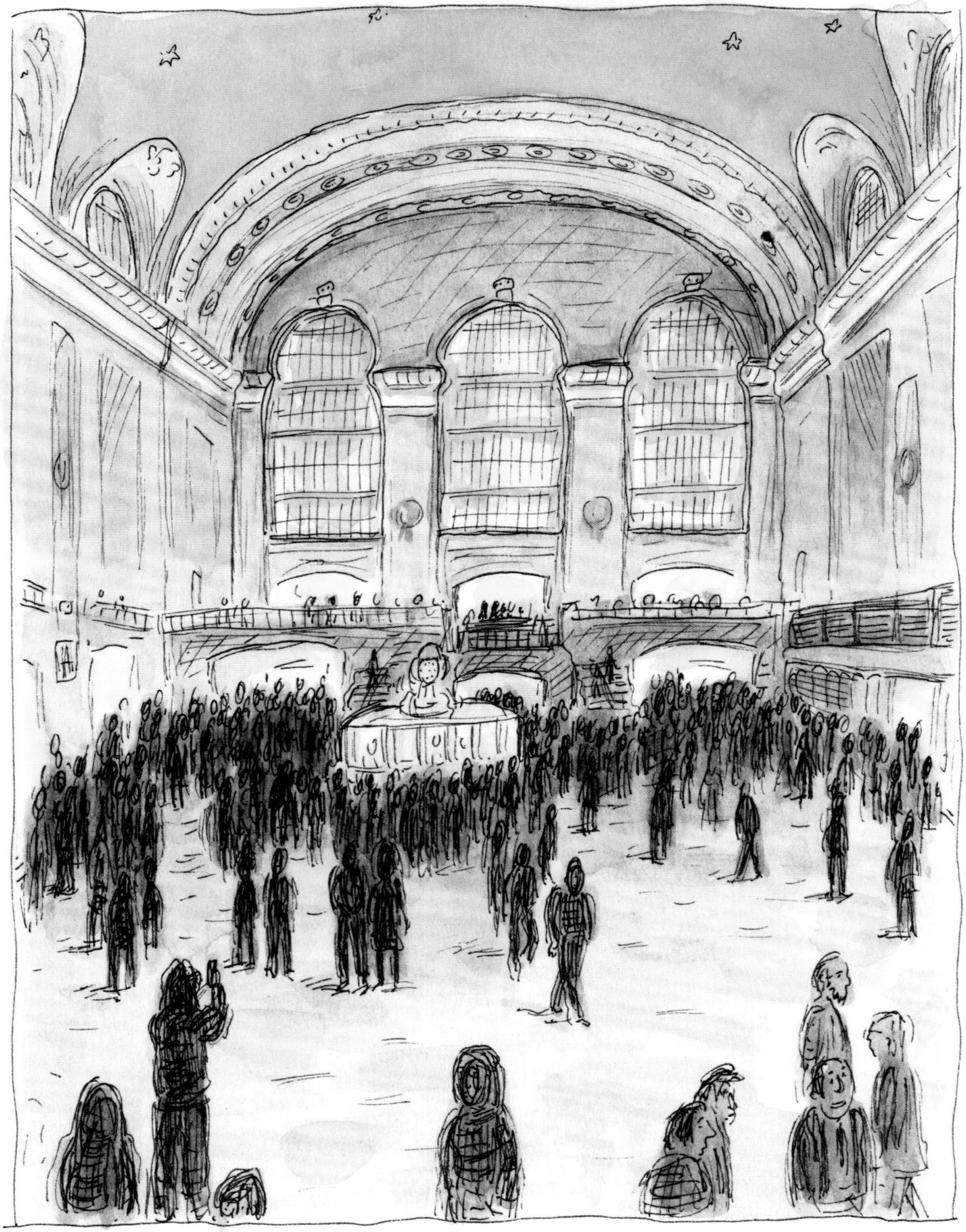

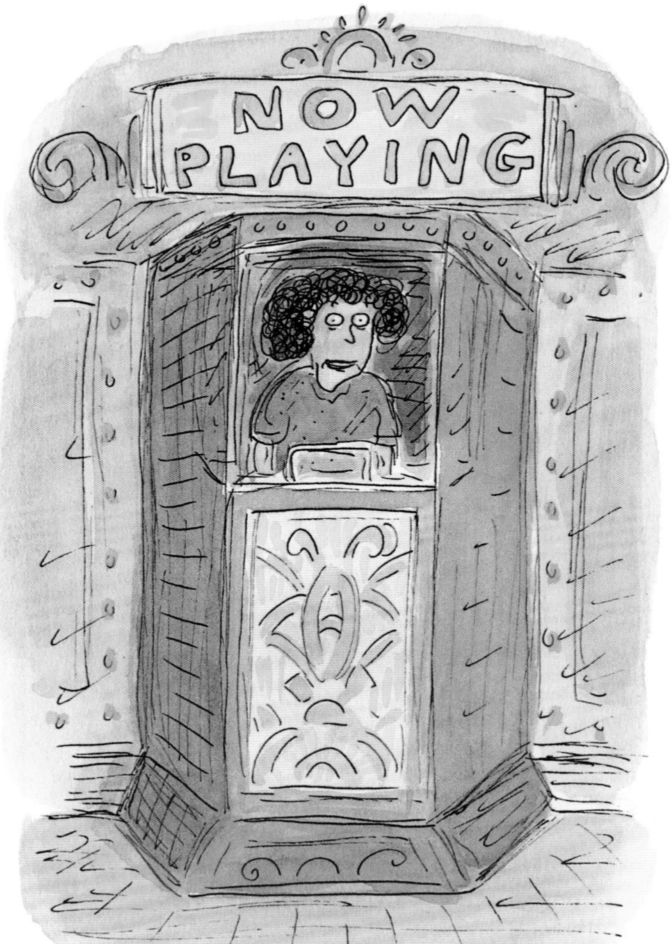
NOW PLAYING

FLORA & FAUNA

6

If you are a fan of wide-open spaces, Manhattan is probably not the place for you. Even when you are outside, it feels like you are inside, possibly because there is not much of a view to the horizon, at least on ground level. This does not bother me. I think of it as "cozy."

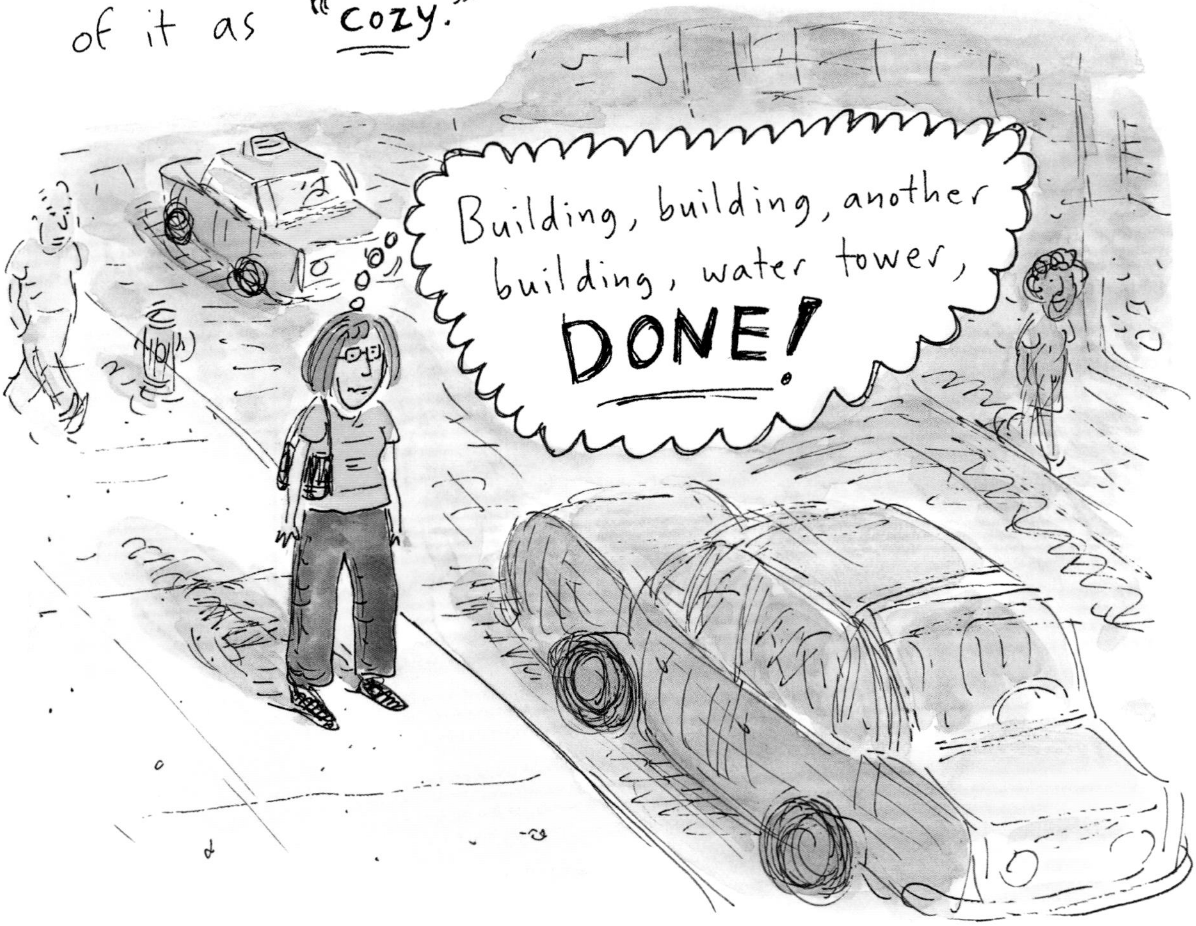
Building, building, another building, water tower, DONE!

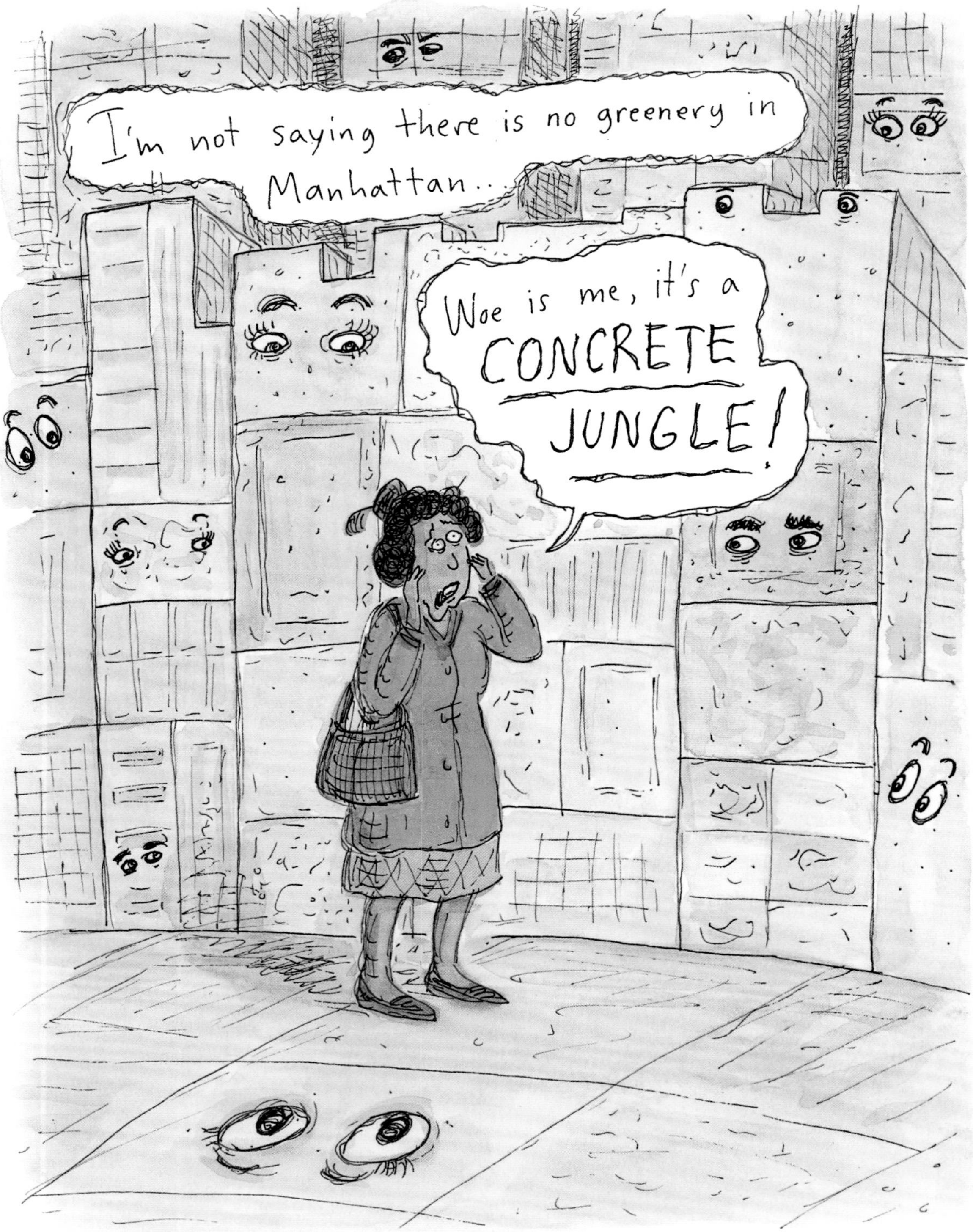
I'm not saying there is no greenery in Manhattan...
Woe is me, it's a CONCRETE JUNGLE!

THERE ARE AT LEAST

70

PARKS HERE.

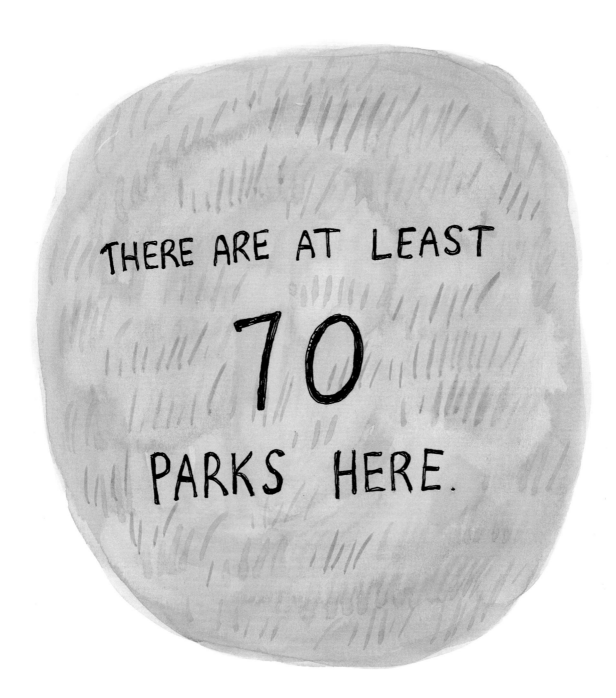

Here are my TOP FIVE:

NAME OF PARK	LOCATION	WHY IT'S GREAT
Bryant Park	Midtown, right behind the New York Public Library. Between 5th and 6th Avenues and 40th and 42nd Streets.	A big square of greenery occupying space that otherwise would contain yet another giant office building or luxury condo tower. I'm o.k. with that.
Fort Tryon Park	Way, way up at the top of Manhattan.	Beautiful, uncrowded, and home to the Cloisters, which houses an amazing collection of medieval art.
Riverside Park	Goes all along the Hudson River from 72nd Street up to 158th Street.	One word: WATERFRONT. Say hello to New Jersey, all the way over there.

NAME OF PARK	LOCATION	WHY IT'S GREAT
The High Line	The Lower West Side - Chelsea. Entrance is near the Whitney Museum - Gansevoort and Washington Streets, but there are multiple points of entry. It continues up to West 30th Street.	This is not a typical meadows-and-lawns park. It's an elevated walkway where you can walk and look at all kinds of plants and shrubs and trees and flowers, and building-scapes and people. It's surprisingly beautiful and satisfying, and its construction and existence is profoundly optimistic about people: that everyone - not just the "elite" - is in need of beauty and wonder.
Central Park	Central Park West to 5th Avenue, West 59th Street to 110th Street.	The CROWN JEWEL OF MANHATTAN...

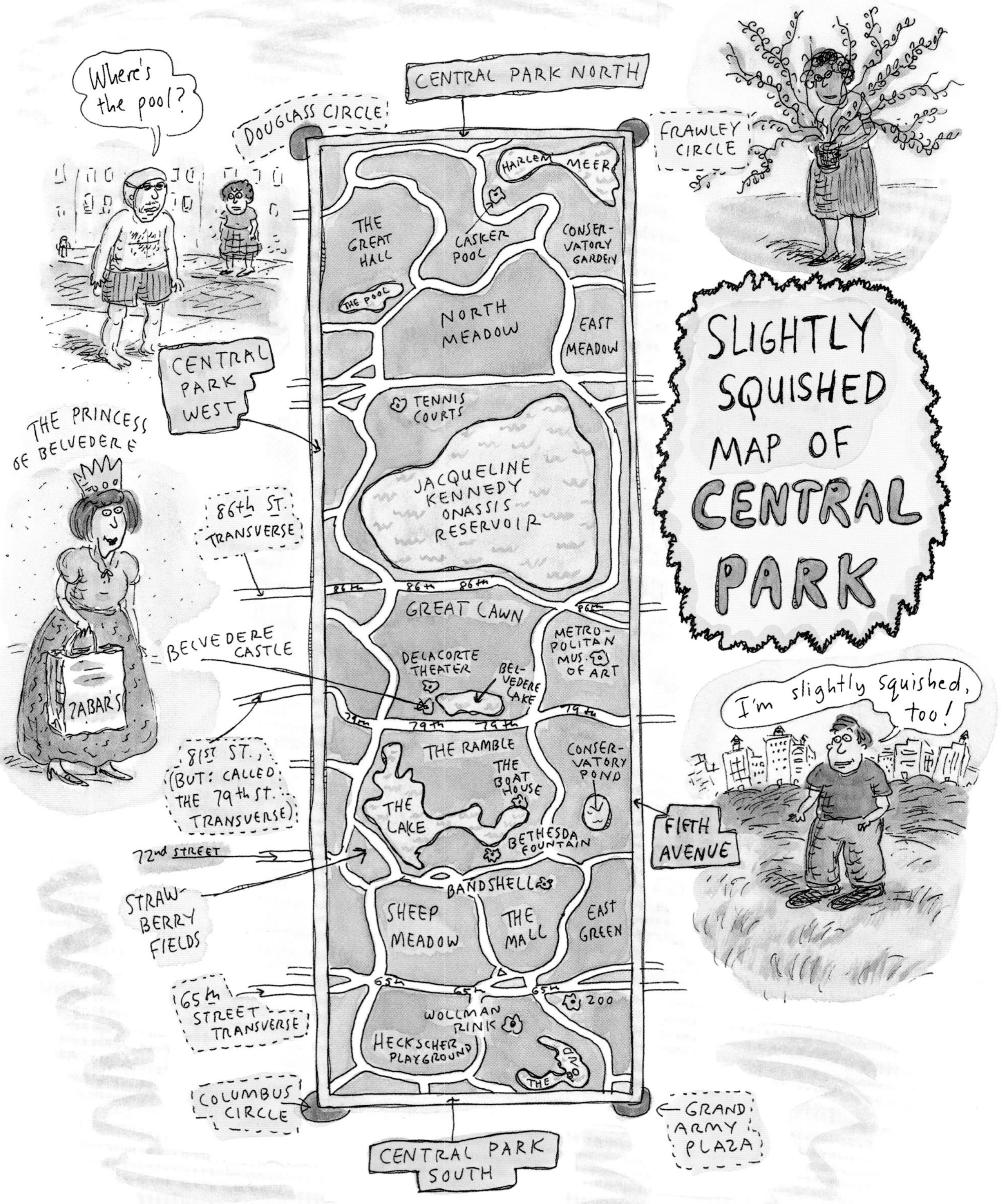

SLIGHTLY SQUISHED MAP OF CENTRAL PARK
Where's the pool?
CENTRAL PARK NORTH
DOUGLASS CIRCLE
FRAWLEY CIRCLE
HARLEM MEER
CASKER POOL
THE GREAT HALL
CONSER-VATORY GARDEN
THE POOL
NORTH MEADOW
EAST MEADOW
CENTRAL PARK WEST
THE PRINCESS OF BELVEDERE
TENNIS COURTS
JACQUELINE KENNEDY ONASSIS RESERVOIR
86th ST. TRANSVERSE
86th
GREAT LAWN
METRO-POLITAN MUS. OF ART
BELVEDERE CASTLE
DELACORTE THEATER
BEL-VEDERE LAKE
ZABAR'S
I'm slightly squished, too!
79th
THE RAMBLE
CONSER-VATORY POND
81st ST., (BUT: CALLED THE 79th ST. TRANSVERSE)
THE BOAT HOUSE
THE LAKE
BETHESDA FOUNTAIN
FIFTH AVENUE
72nd STREET
BANDSHELL
STRAW-BERRY FIELDS
SHEEP MEADOW
THE MALL
EAST GREEN
65th
65th STREET TRANSVERSE
ZOO
WOLLMAN RINK
HECKSCHER PLAYGROUND
THE POND
COLUMBUS CIRCLE
GRAND ARMY PLAZA
CENTRAL PARK SOUTH

Of all the parks in Manhattan, Central Park—which covers 6% of the borough's total acreage—is my favorite. It contains lots of Nature, but is no more "natural" than an arrangement of flowers from your neighborhood florist. It was designed specifically for the pleasure of the public—i.e., YOU—by Frederick Law Olmsted and Calvert Vaux, who won a park-design competition in 1858. Olmsted said that the park was "of great importance as the first real park made in this country—a democratic development of the highest significance."

OLMSTED   VAUX

THANK YOU

Central Park contains meadows, trees, paths, bridges, bodies of water, boats, a bandshell, playgrounds, ball fields, benches, lamp posts, dense areas of brambles, jumbles of rocks, turtles, a merry-go-round, a skating rink, statues, a castle, a zoo, restaurants, an incredible number of birds including flocks of escaped parakeets ~

I saw an open window, and _that was_ _all she wrote_!

~ and much, MUCH, MUCH, MUCH MORE.

Central Park offers its visitors all of the benefits of a walk in Nature - fresh air, sky, trees, grass, space, etc. - with none of its drawbacks:

Getting lost...
Where ARE we?!?
No idea. No idea IN HELL.
Troublesome wildlife...
Running out of food and water...
Sorry.
That's o.k.

Without Central Park, Manhattan would be unlivable. It really would be a "concrete jungle."

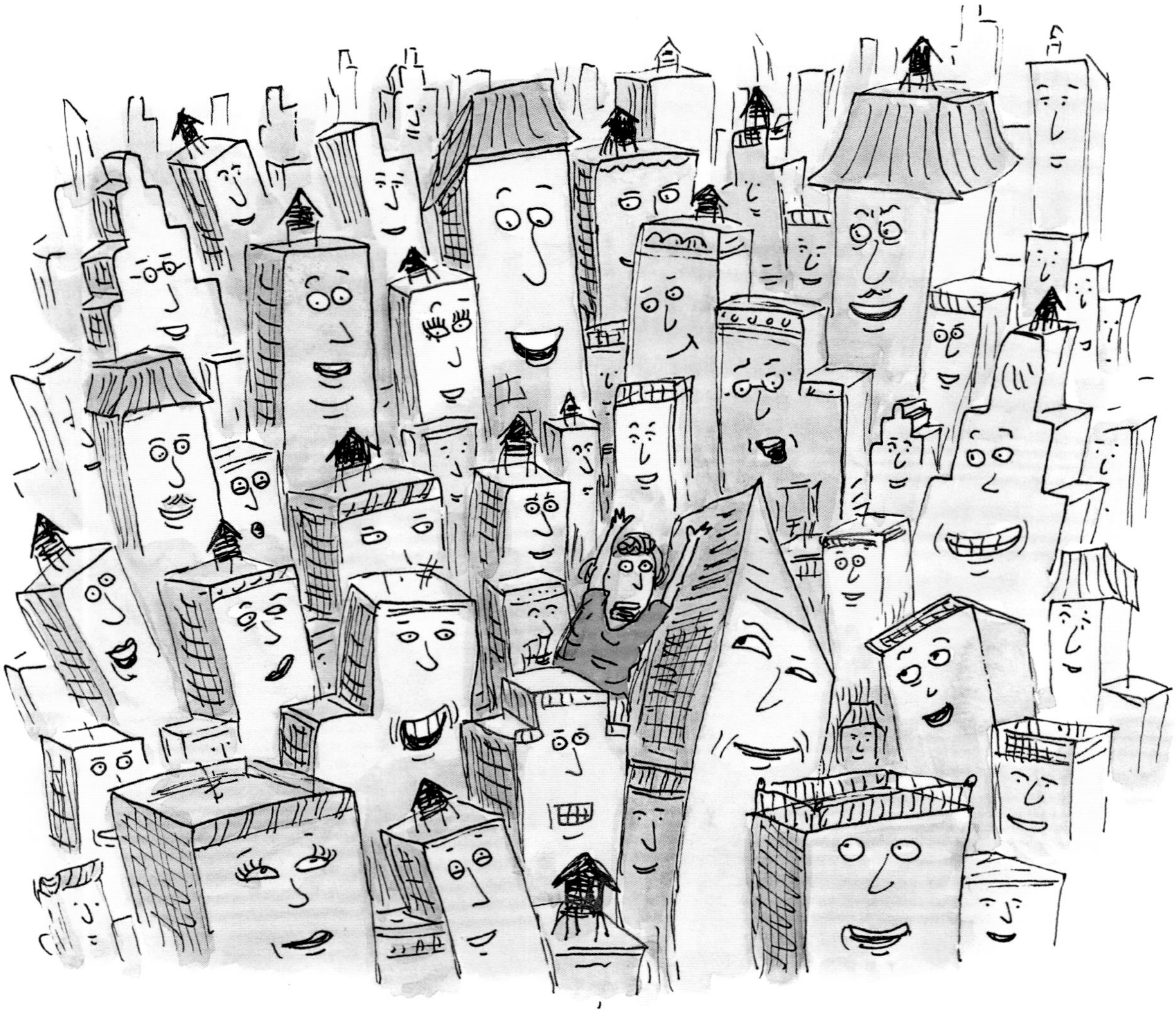

However, the wonders of Nature are not limited to the city's parks.

A SELECTION OF MANHATTAN WILDLIFE

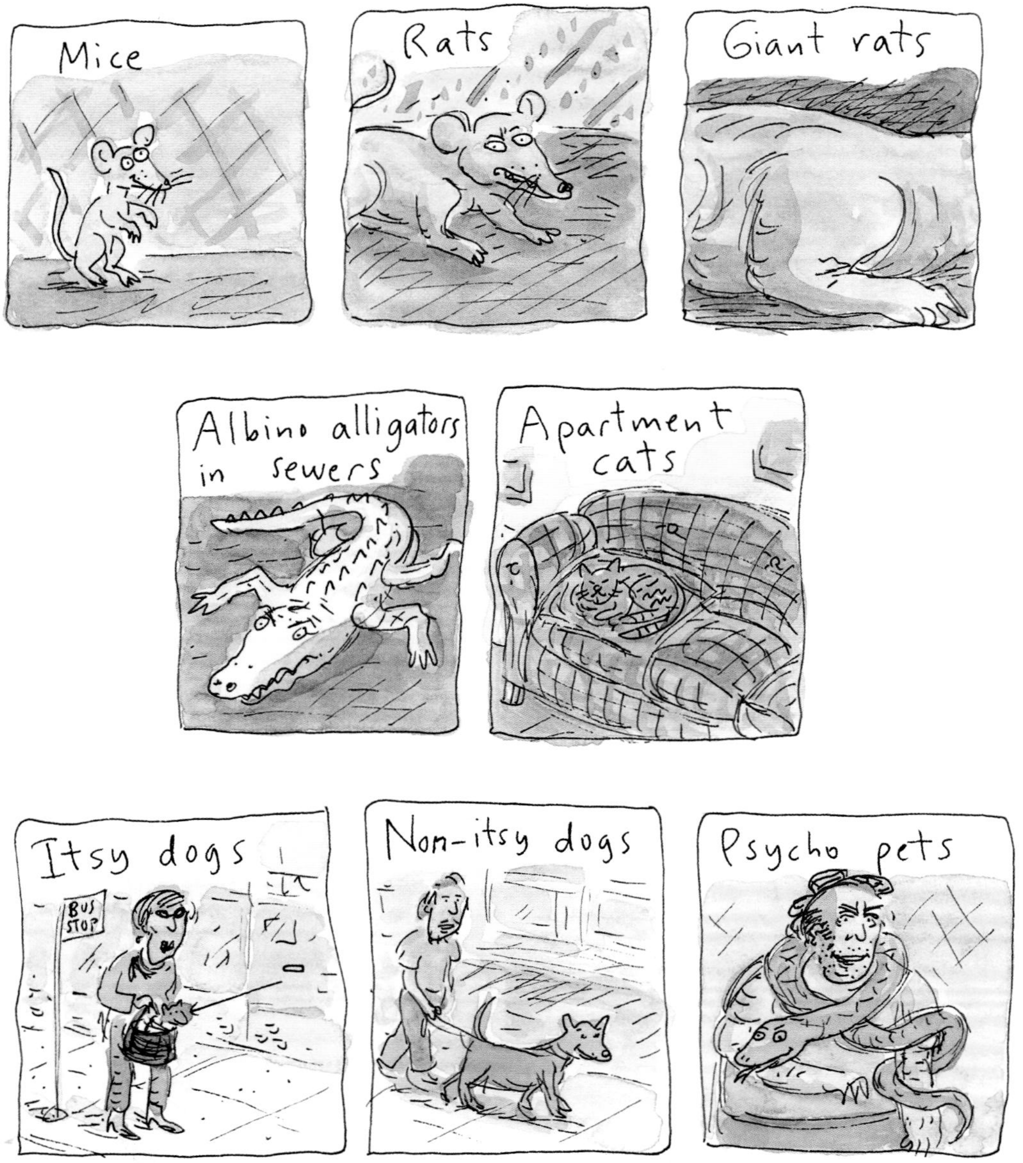

Mice
Rats
Giant rats
Albino alligators in sewers
Apartment cats
Itsy dogs
BUS STOP
Non-itsy dogs
Psycho pets

But the main wildlife in Manhattan is probably insects: cockroaches, bedbugs, silverfish, etc. I still remember the first time I saw a waterbug*. He was walking along 14th Street, just like any other pedestrian.

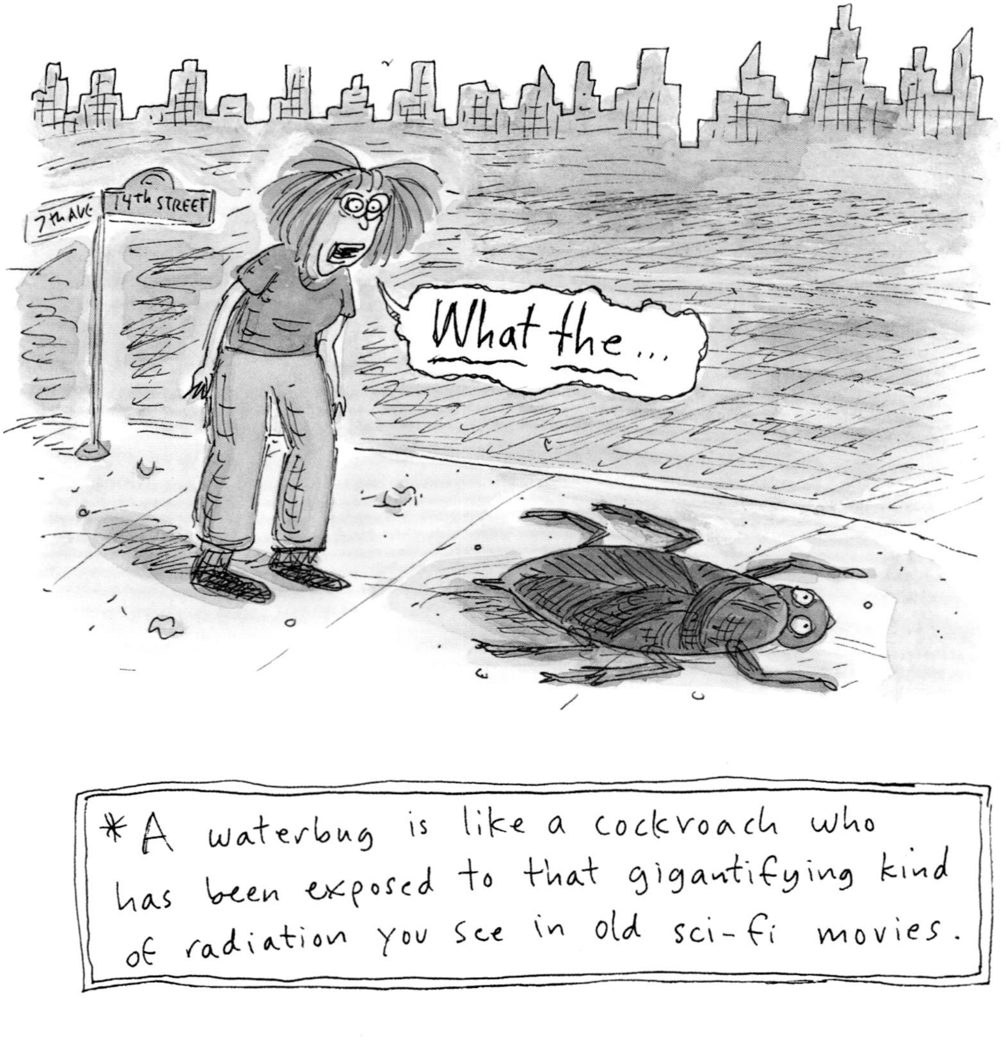
7th AVE
14th STREET
What the...

*A waterbug is like a cockroach who has been exposed to that gigantifying kind of radiation you see in old sci-fi movies.

In New York, bugs live inside more than they live outside. If you have an *infestation*, don't panic. Tell your super. He'll arrange for an exterminator to come to your apartment. Chances are, you'll need him to come more than once. Maybe every month. Look! You've made a new friend!

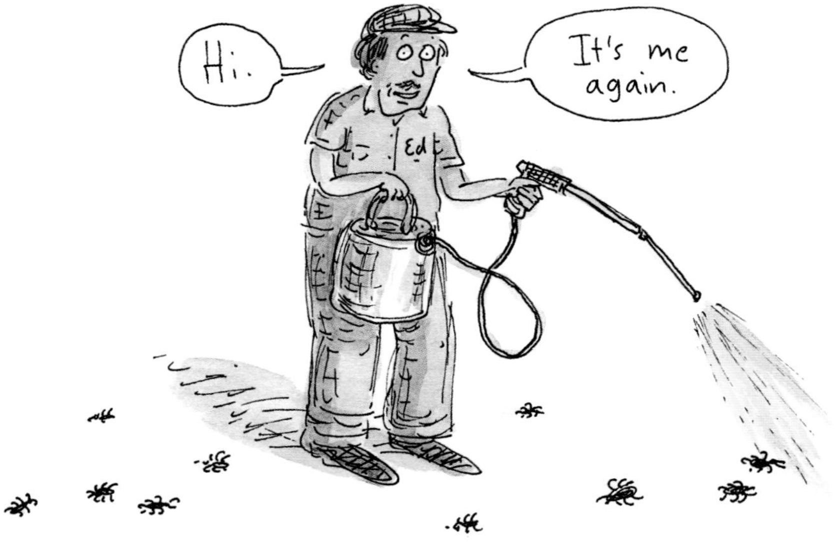
Hi.
It's me again.
Ed

Bedbugs are even worse. Don't invite them into your apartment by picking up that cute, discarded, **BEDBUG-COLONIZED THROW PILLOW** you see on the street.

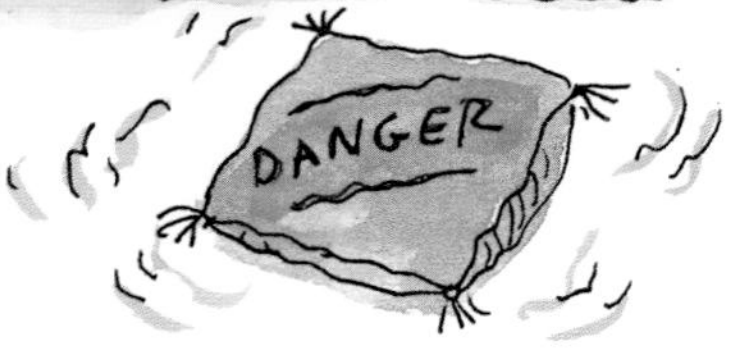
DANGER

The most common **four**-legged animals you'll see on the street are household pets. Mostly dogs. Not cats, who tend to prefer sofas to sidewalks...

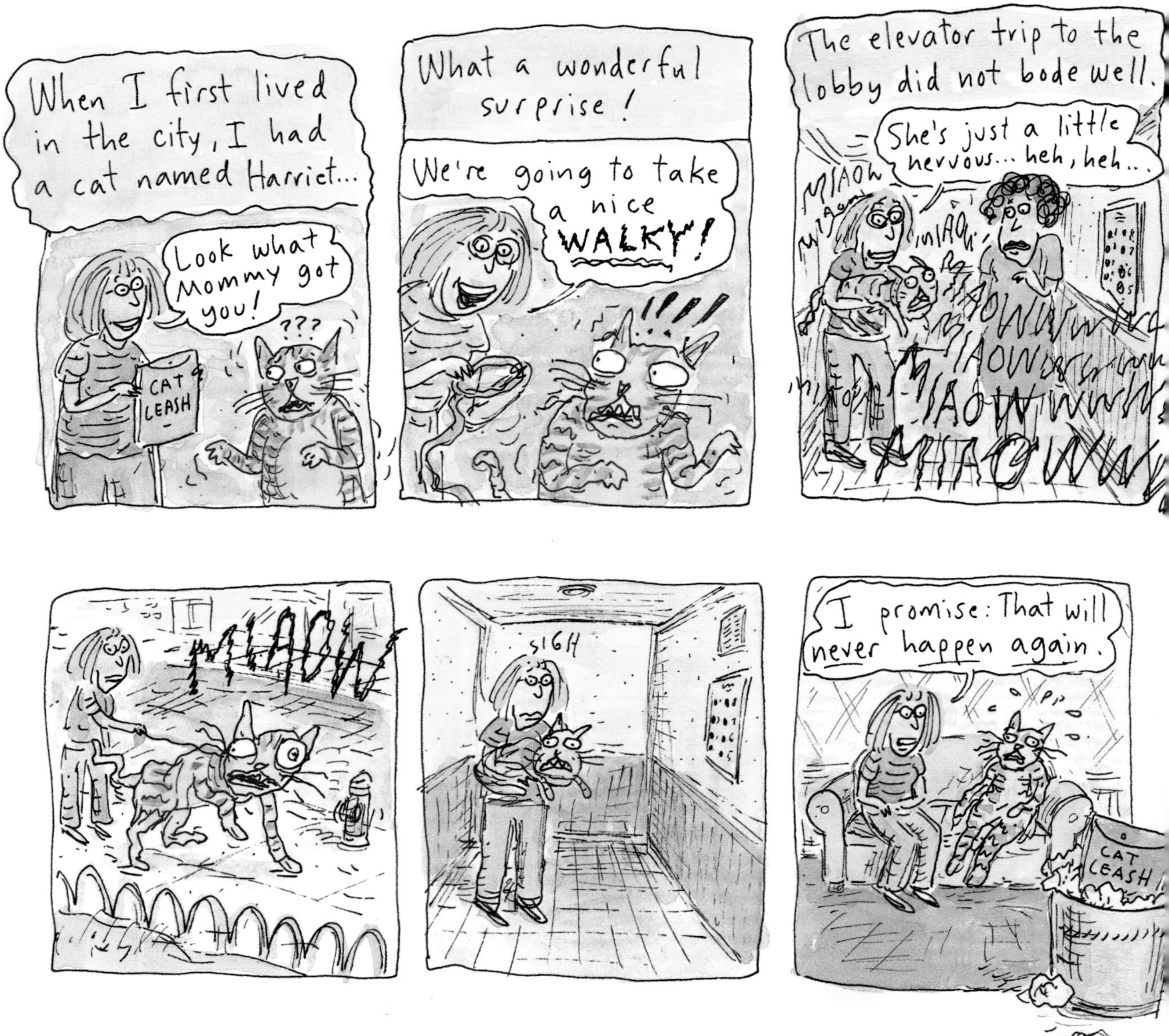
When I first lived in the city, I had a cat named Harriet...
Look what Mommy got you!
???
CAT LEASH
What a wonderful surprise!
We're going to take a nice WALKY!
The elevator trip to the lobby did not bode well.
She's just a little nervous... heh, heh...
MIAOW
MIAOW
MIAOW
SIGH
I promise: That will never happen again.
CAT LEASH

If Manhattan had an official tree, it would be this one:

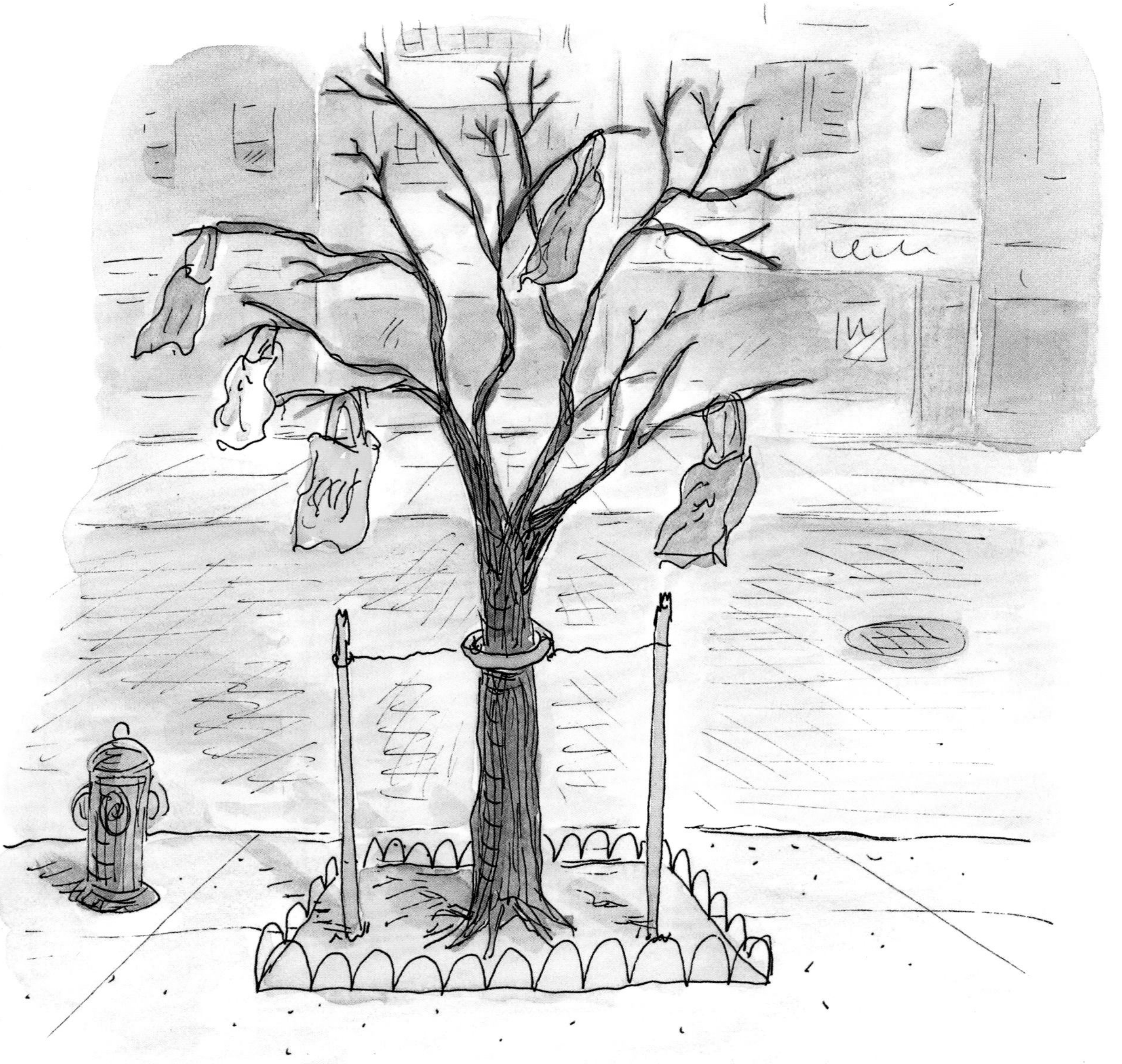

If Manhattan had an official animal, it would be the pigeon...

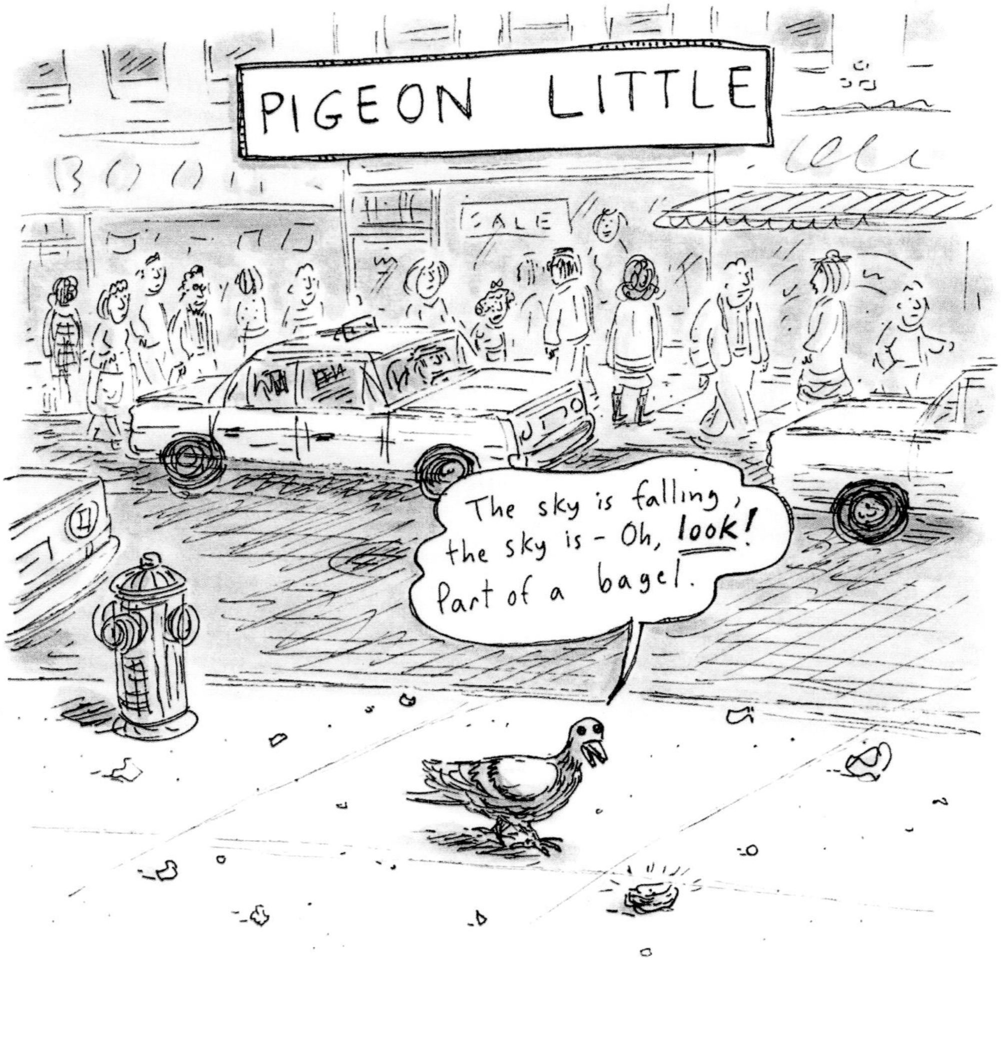
PIGEON LITTLE
SALE
The sky is falling, the sky is - Oh, look! Part of a bagel.

Speaking of pigeons, perhaps you're feeling **PECKISH**...

7

FOOD

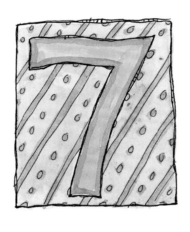

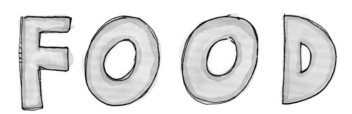

One of the most pleasant things
about Manhattan, as opposed to say, Death
Valley, is the unlikelihood that you will
run out of food or water.

My father used to carry a little bit of
food with him when he went into town—

a banana

a wax paper
bag with a piece
of honeycake in it

a plastic
bag containing
a stack of
graham crackers

At some point, he'd announce to my mother:

Elizabeth, I feel like chewing on something.

And then out would come the honeycake or whatever. My mother HATED when he used that expression—"chewing on something"— but he used it all the time anyway. There are worse things to fight about. Probably.

One thing neither of them ever brought with them was WATER. That was because back in the Olden Days, people didn't need to hydrate themselves every fifteen minutes. Who knows why this was?!? It's a medical mystery.

But don't feel as if you have to carry around your own personal roast chicken. Food is one thing Manhattan is not short of, from your-monthly-rent = dinner (not including drinks) type places to the humblest sidewalk stand.

JOE'S DIRTY-WATER DOGS

My default restaurant is the coffee shop, also sometimes called the diner. Why? Because if you stick to basics, like grilled cheese or eggs, YOU CANNOT GO TOO WRONG. Sure, a daredevil might order Sushi Enchiladas, but that doesn't mean *you* have to.

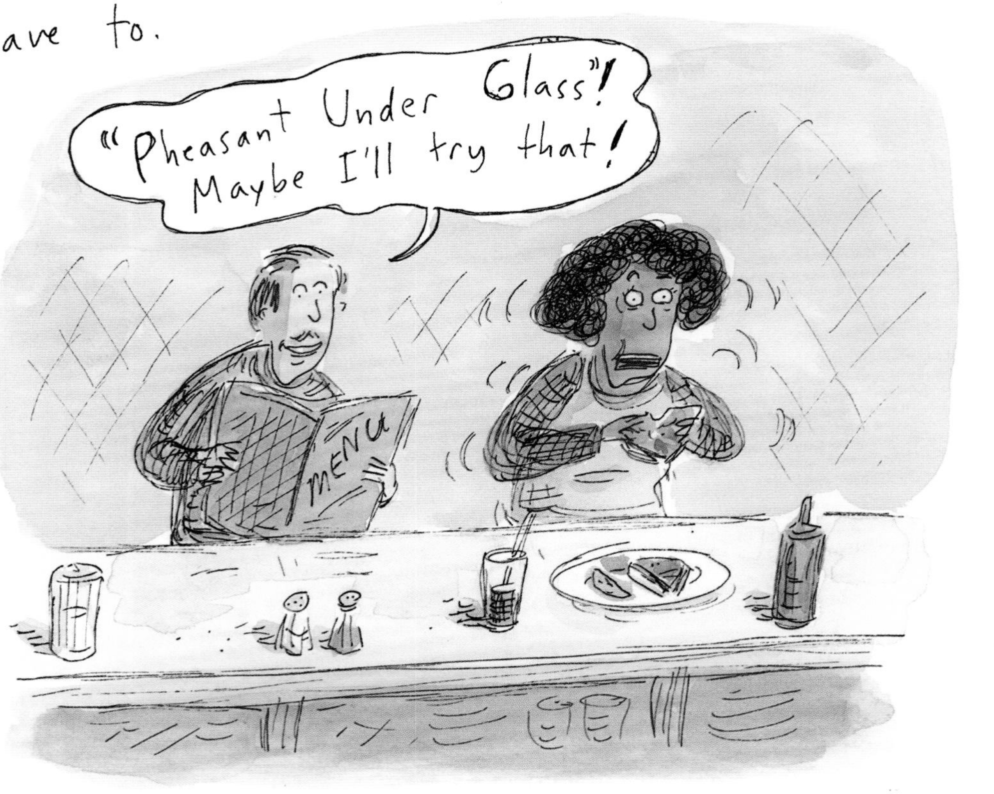
"Pheasant Under Glass"! Maybe I'll try that!
MENU

Many diners/coffee shops are open 24 hours a day, 7 days a week. You won't be the only person who needs some french toast at four A.M. And if you are, nobody cares.

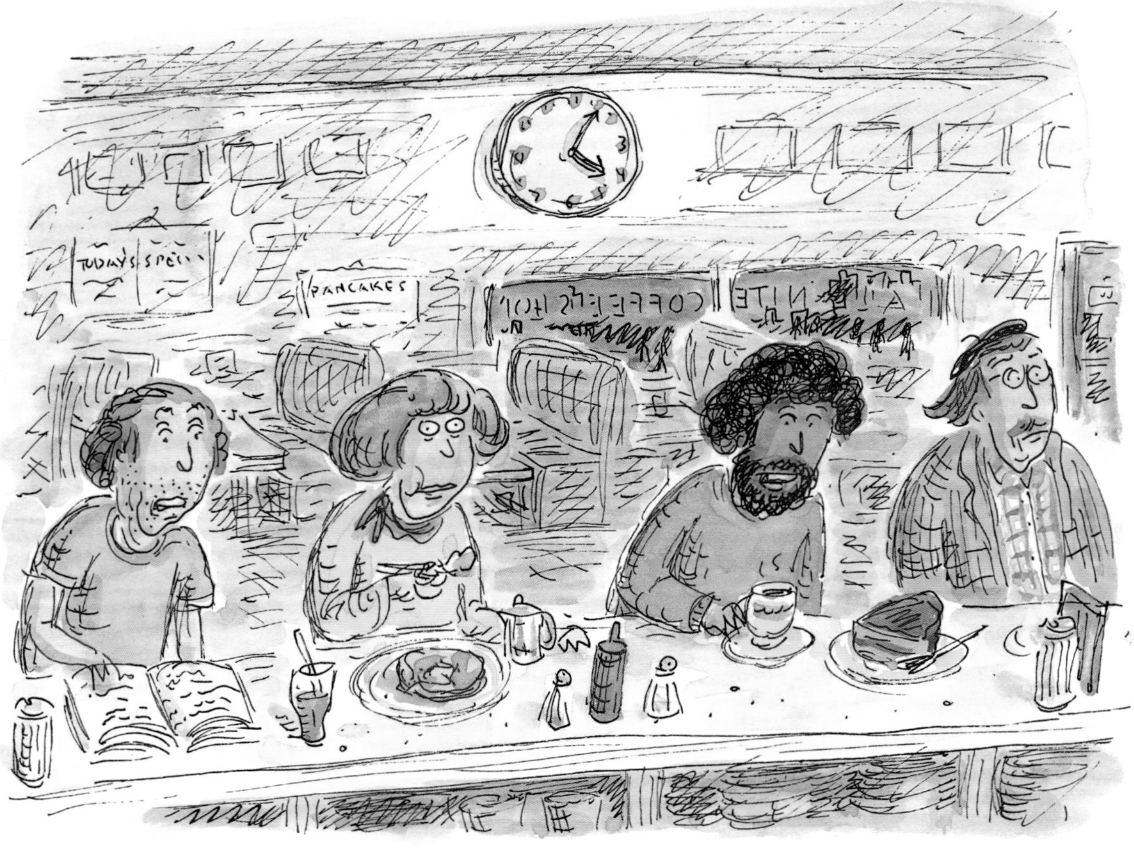
PANCAKES

In Manhattan, every food ethnicity, preference,
above is represented. If you can't find what you

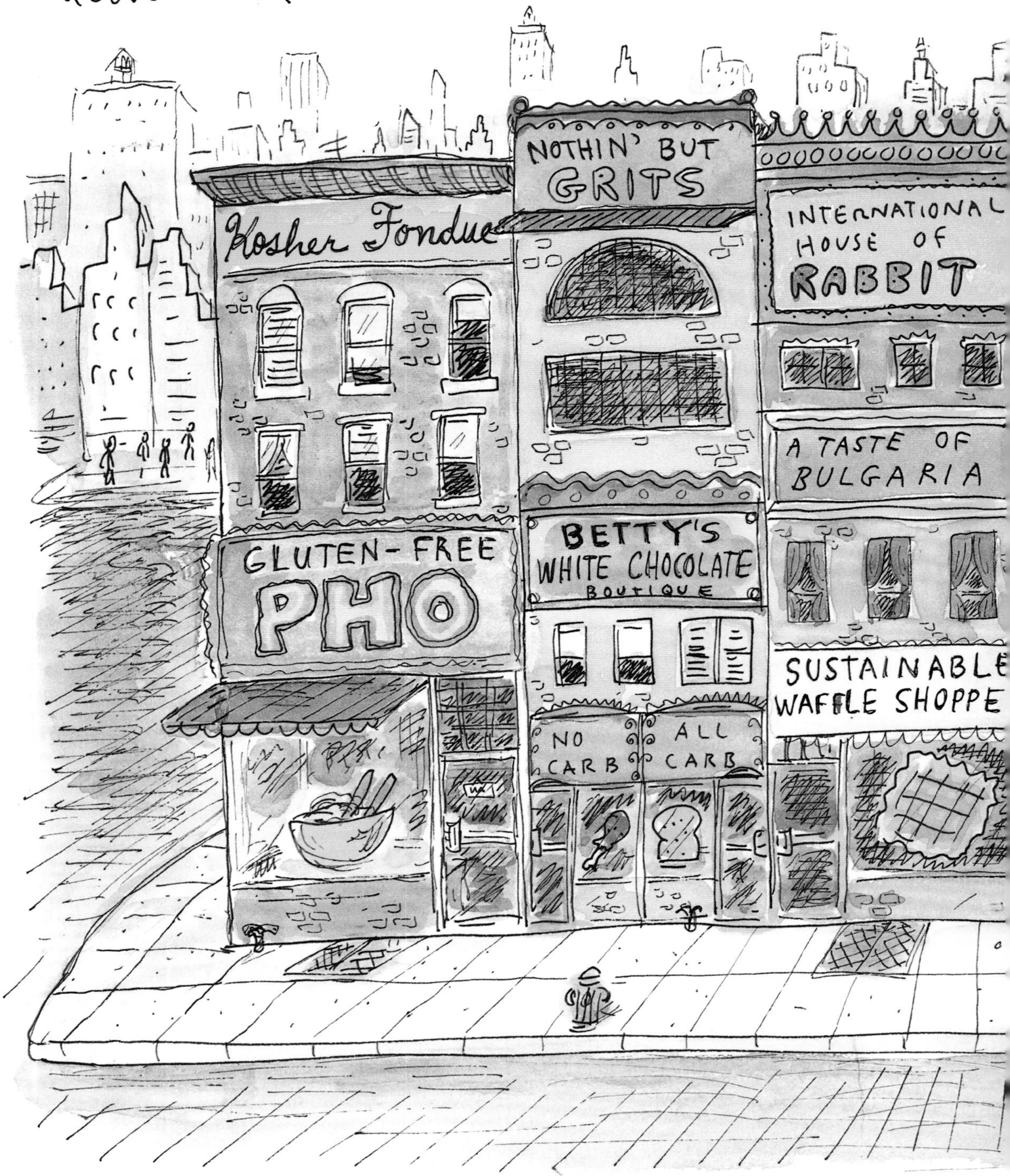
Kosher Fondue
NOTHIN' BUT GRITS
INTERNATIONAL HOUSE OF RABBIT
A TASTE OF BULGARIA
GLUTEN-FREE PHO
BETTY'S WHITE CHOCOLATE BOUTIQUE
SUSTAINABLE WAFFLE SHOPPE
NO CARB
ALL CARB

aversion, allergy, craving, fad, or combination of the want to eat here, maybe you don't like food.

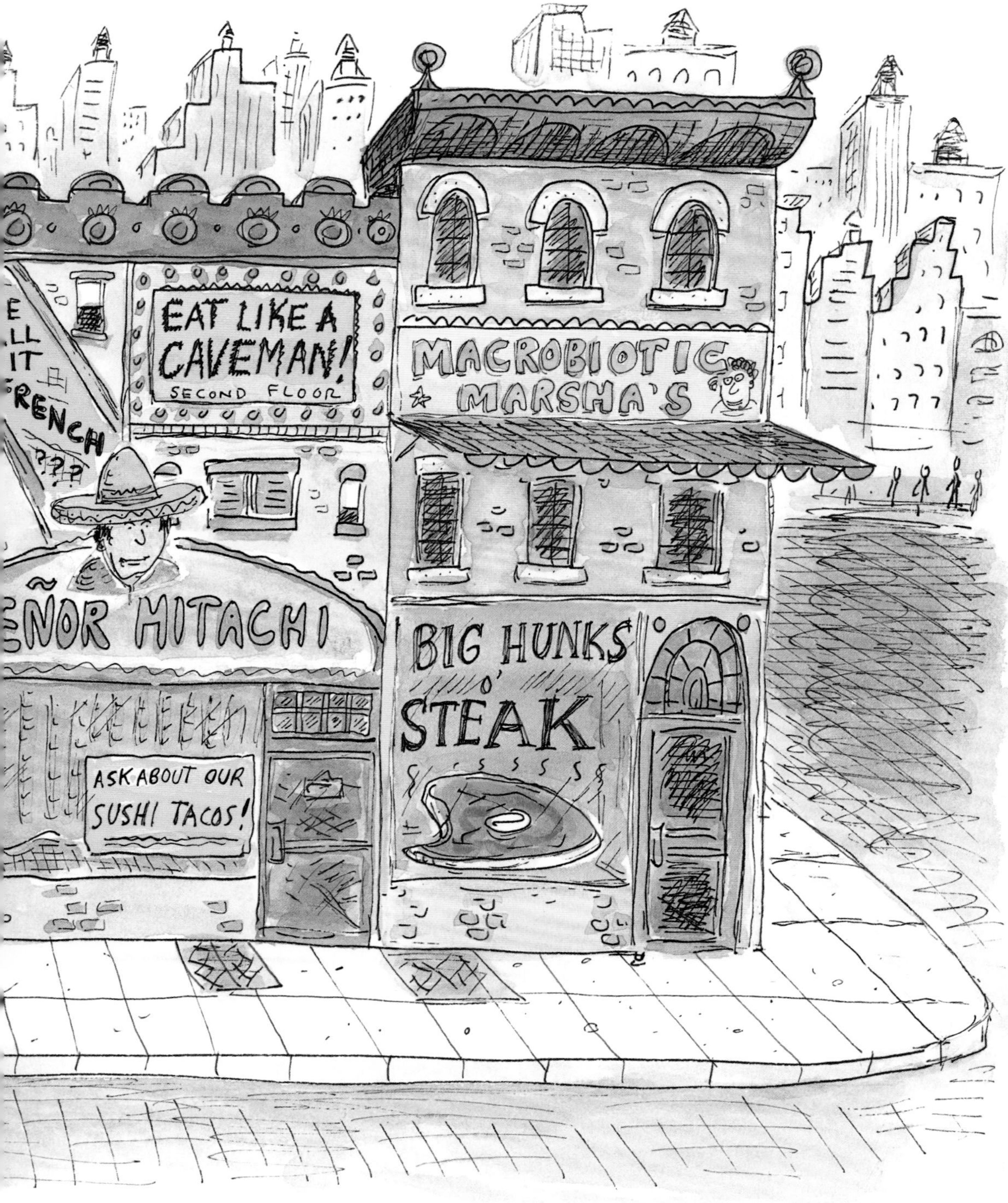

EAT LIKE A CAVEMAN!
SECOND FLOOR
MACROBIOTIC MARSHA'S
ÑOR HITACHI
ASK ABOUT OUR SUSHI TACOS!
BIG HUNKS O' STEAK
RENCH
???

And for those days for whatever reason you can't or won't leave the apartment, and you can't or won't cook, there's always delivery.

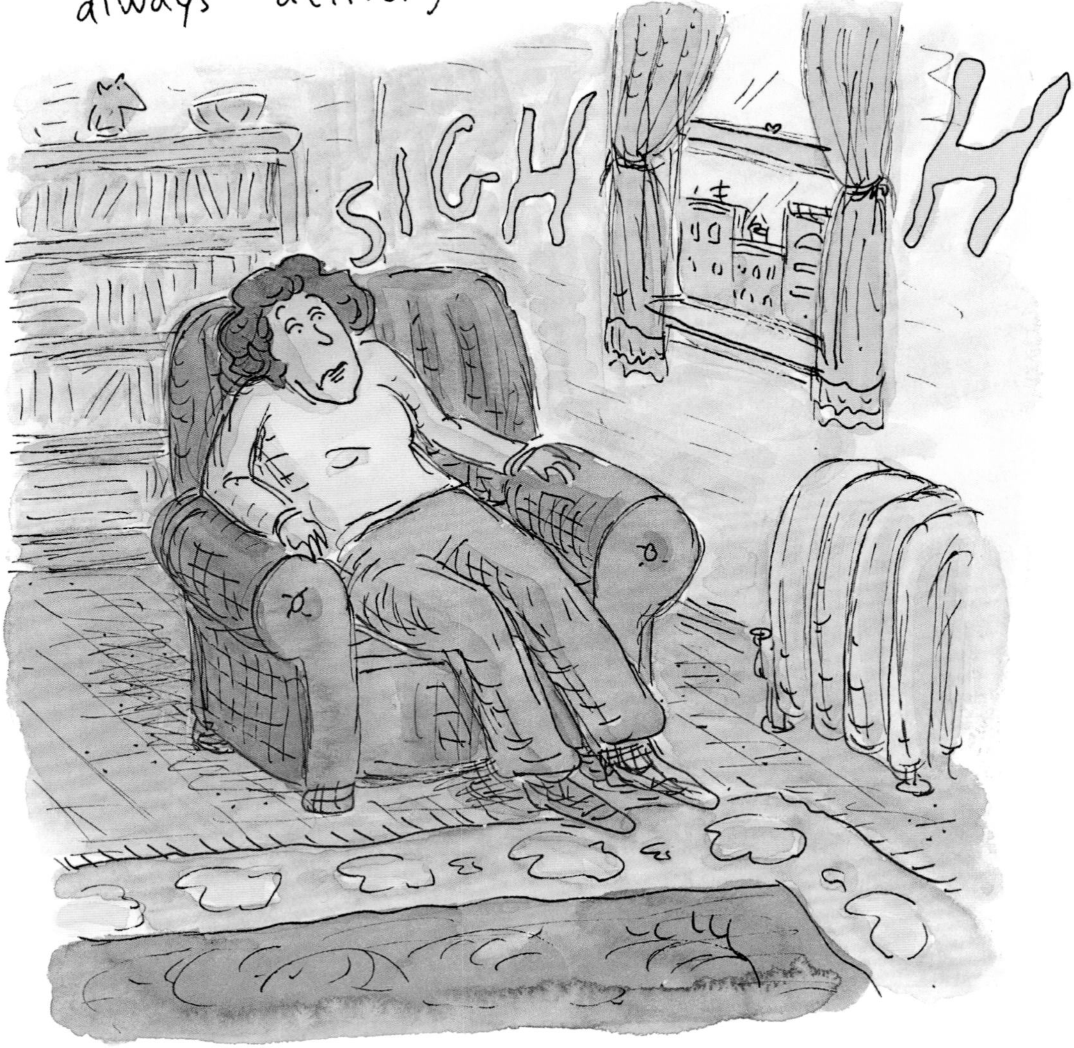
SIGHHH

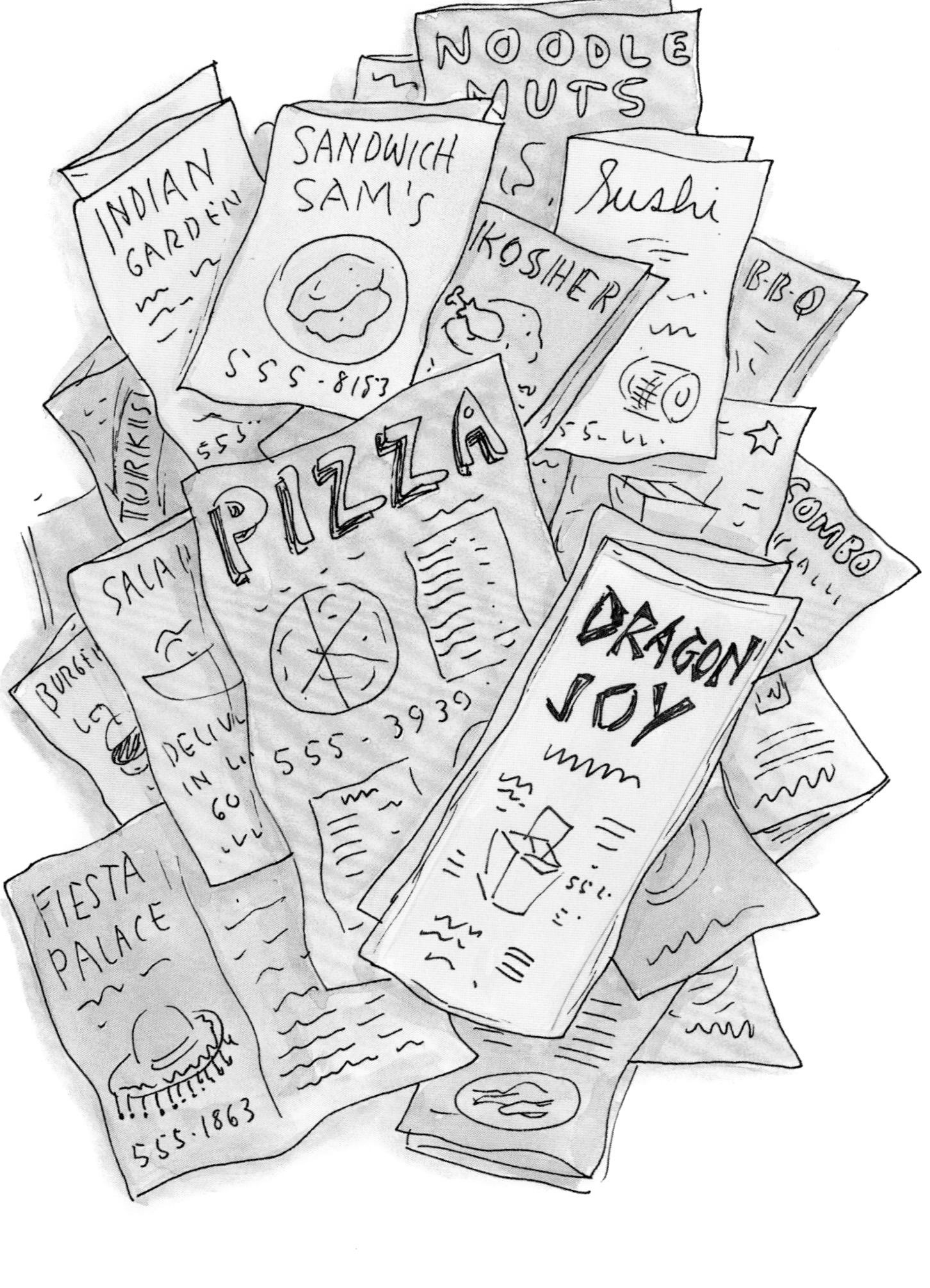
NOODLE NUTS
SANDWICH SAM'S
555-8153
INDIAN GARDEN
KOSHER
Sushi
BBQ
PIZZA
555-3939
DRAGON JOY
FIESTA PALACE
555-1863

A Starbucks Reverie

OVERHEARD IN THE FIELD

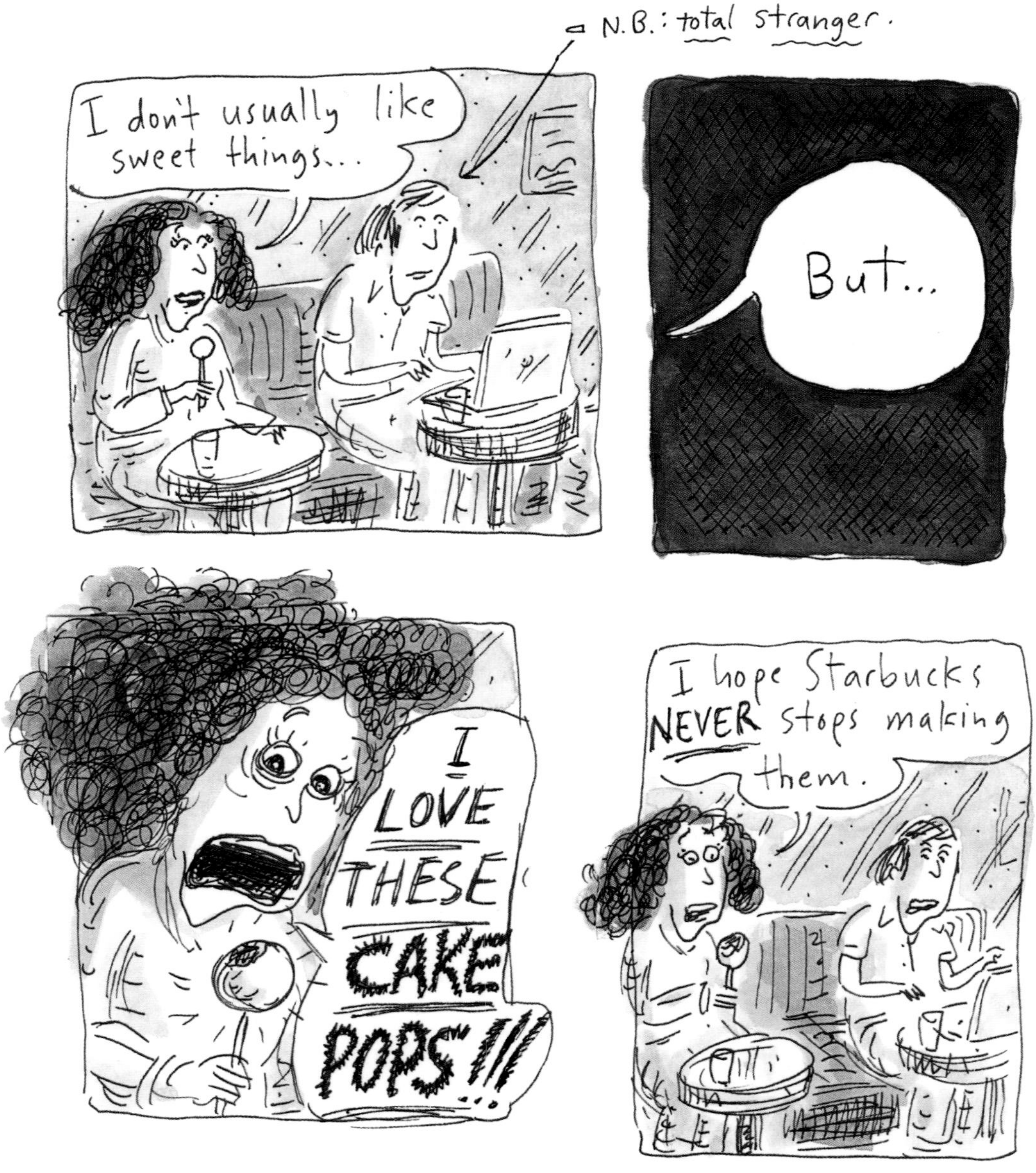
N.B.: total stranger.
I don't usually like sweet things...
But...
I LOVE THESE CAKE POPS!!!
I hope Starbucks NEVER stops making them.

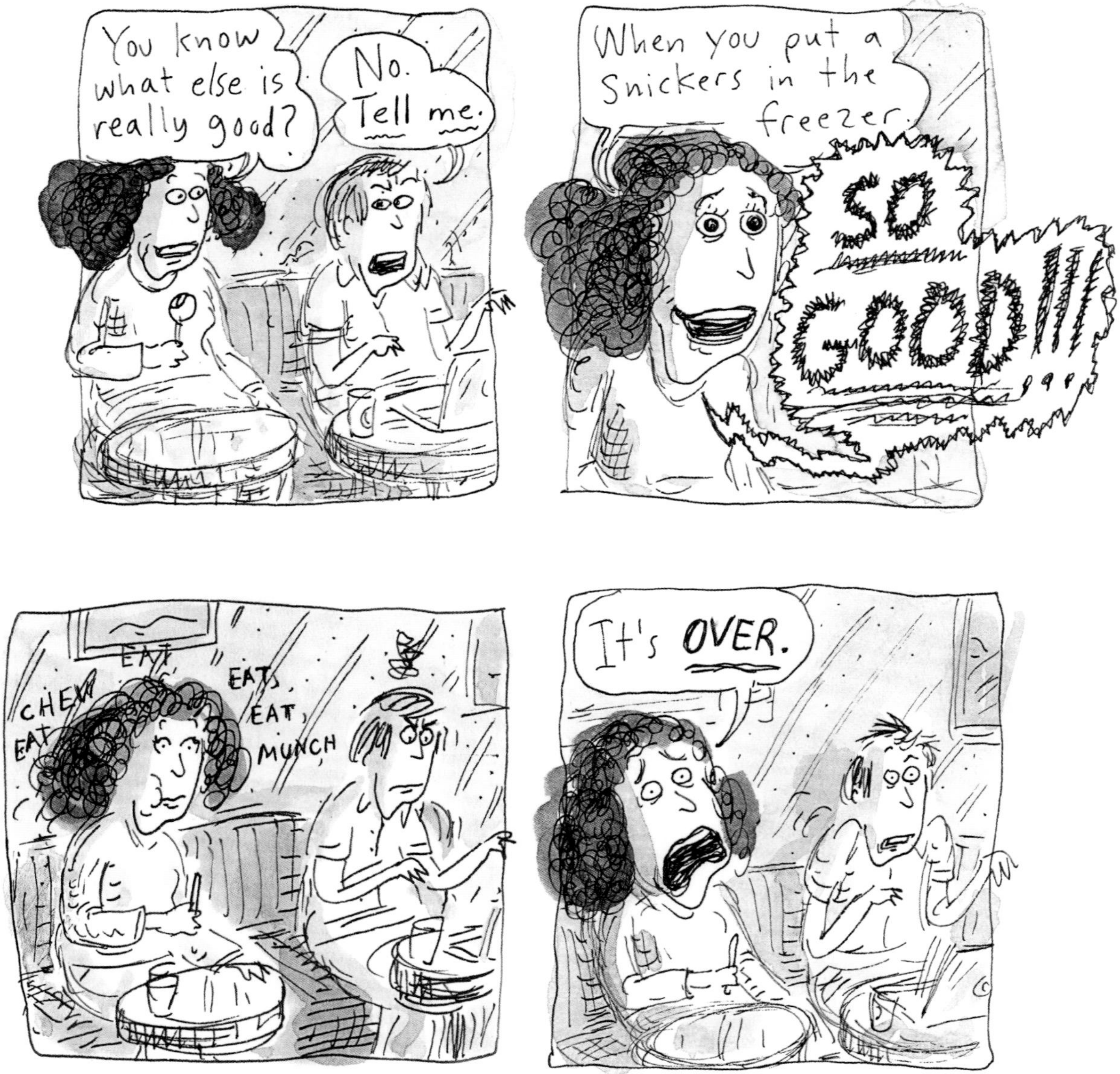

You know what else is really good?
No. Tell me.
When you put a Snickers in the freezer.
SO GOOD!!!
EAT
CHEW
EAT
EAT
EAT
MUNCH
It's OVER.

So: you've walked around. You've gone places and looked at stuff: parks, museums, people around you. Maybe you've had it, and you want to go back to wherever you came from. Be my guest.

But perhaps you've decided that this is where you need to live, come hell or high water...

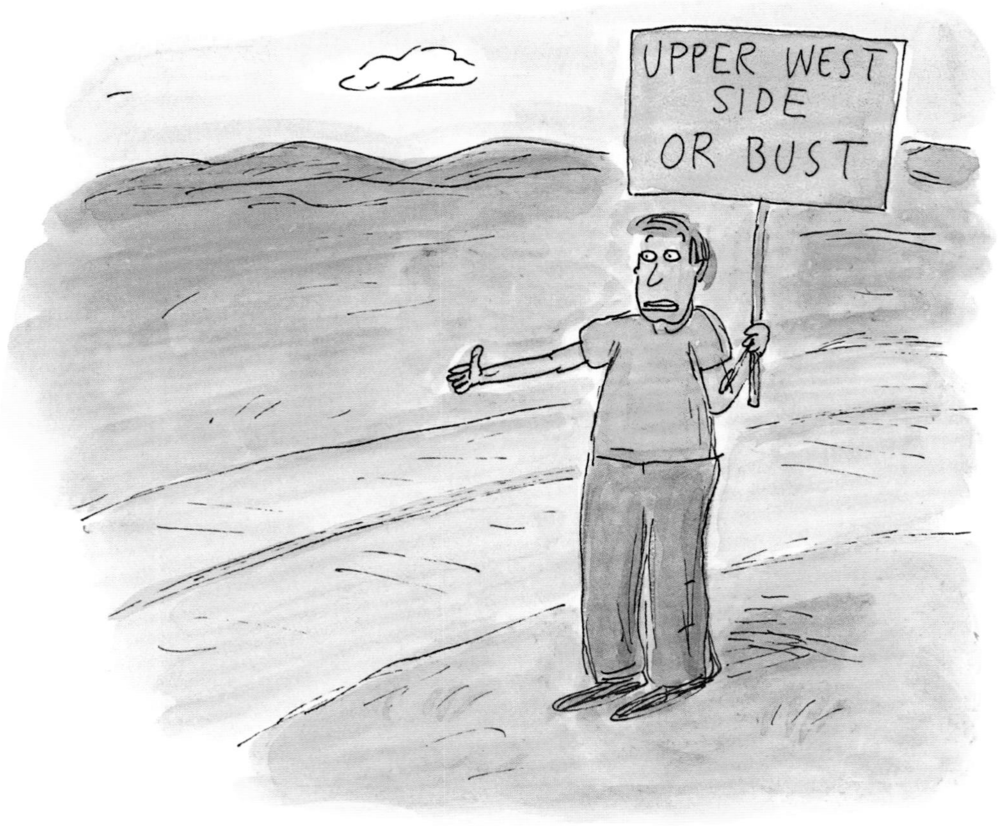
UPPER WEST SIDE OR BUST

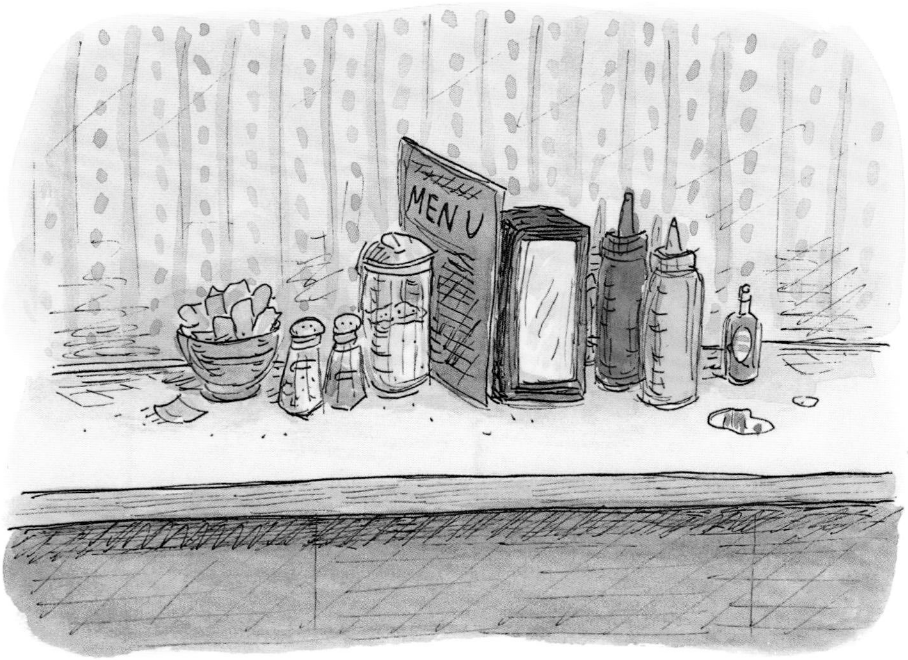
MENU

8

APARTMENTS

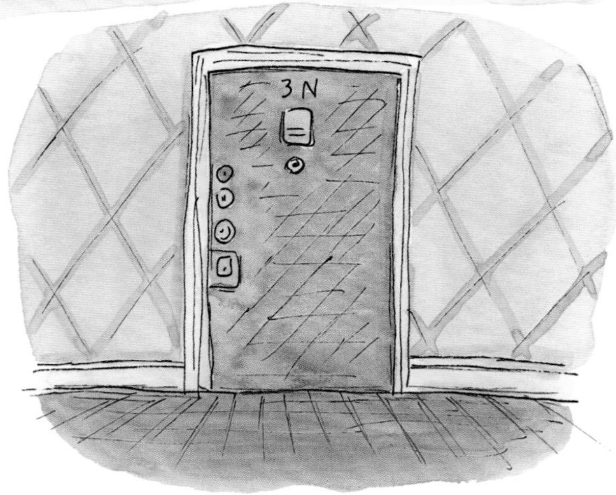
3N

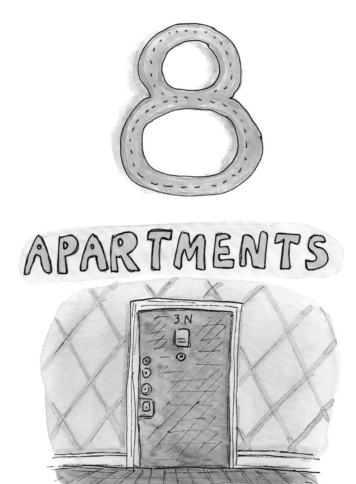

One of the first noticeable things about Manhattan is that there are almost no private houses.

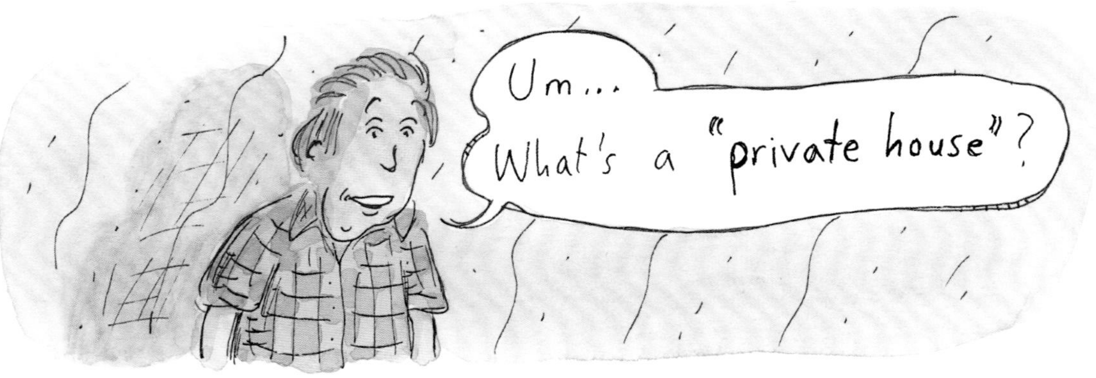
Um...
What's a "private house"?

A "private house" is what mainland America calls a "house." It's the opposite of "apartment." In Brooklyn, where I grew up, kids asked each other:

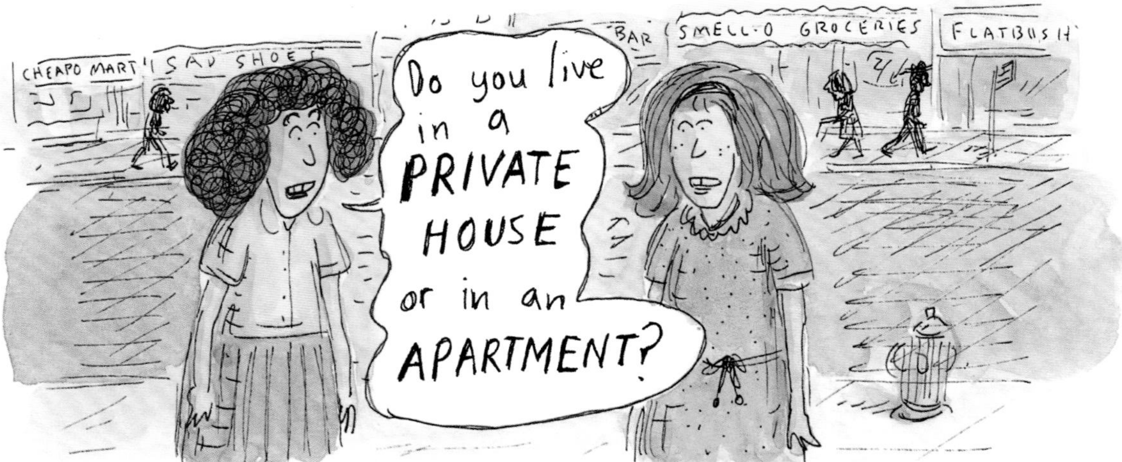
CHEAPO MART
SAD SHOE
BAR
SMELL-O GROCERIES
FLATBUSH
Do you live in a PRIVATE HOUSE or in an APARTMENT?

When you first move here, you will experience several different kinds of apartments.

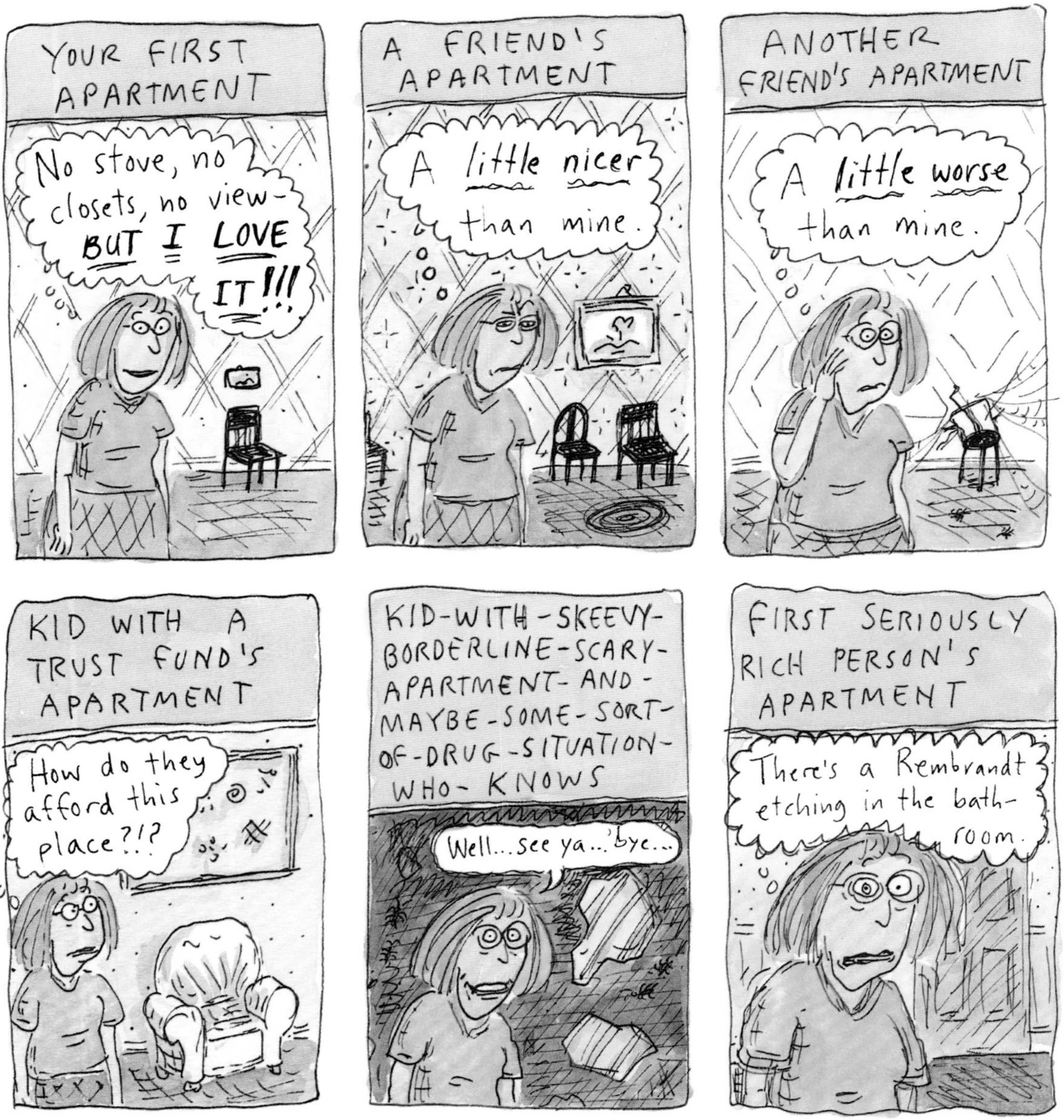
YOUR FIRST APARTMENT
No stove, no closets, no view- BUT I LOVE IT!!!
A FRIEND'S APARTMENT
A little nicer than mine.
ANOTHER FRIEND'S APARTMENT
A little worse than mine.
KID WITH A TRUST FUND'S APARTMENT
How do they afford this place?!?
KID-WITH-SKEEVY-BORDERLINE-SCARY-APARTMENT-AND-MAYBE-SOME-SORT-OF-DRUG-SITUATION-WHO-KNOWS
Well... see ya...'bye...
FIRST SERIOUSLY RICH PERSON'S APARTMENT
There's a Rembrandt etching in the bath-room.

There are pros and cons about apartment life.

When I was a kid, my mother used to keep a crutch handy, so when the horrible upstairs neighbors, who had clearly never lived in an apartment house before, started riding their horses or whatever they were doing, she could bang on the ceiling with it. It didn't always work.

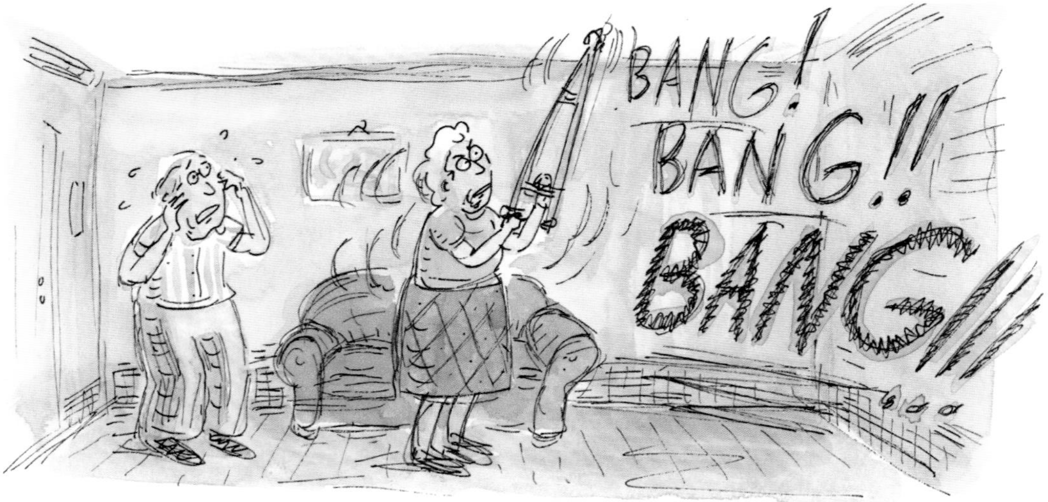
BANG!
BANG!!
BANG!!

Living in an apartment with people on both sides and above and below, is different from living in a house. Essentially, one does one's best not to be a jerk. Don't practice your saxophone after ten p.m. and I won't move my furniture around in the middle of the night.

AND WHEN ALL ELSE FAILS:

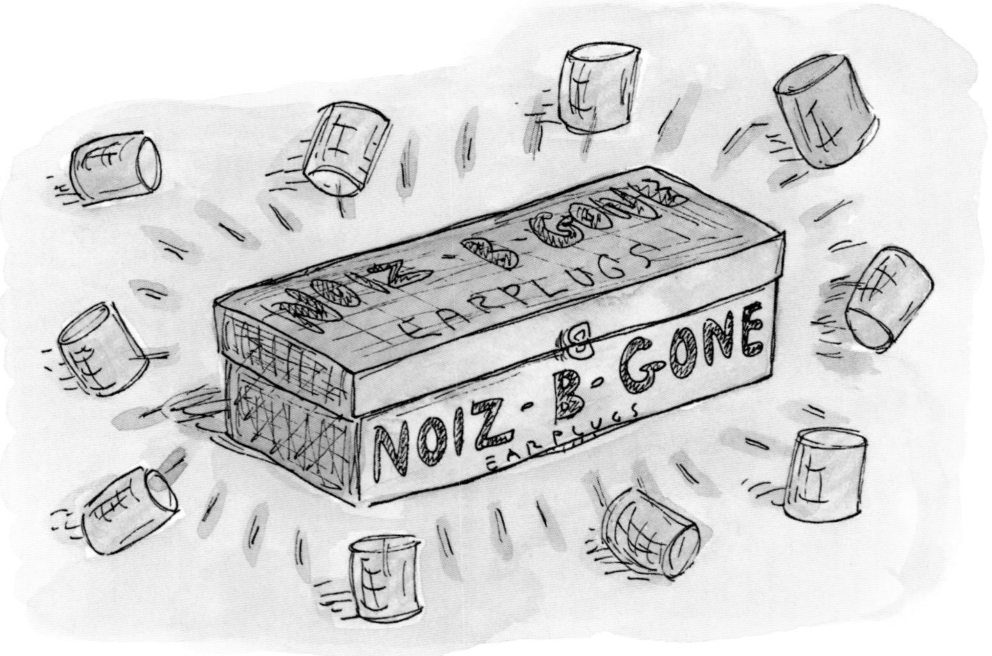
NOIZ-B-GONE
EARPLUGS
NOIZ-B-GONE
EARPLUGS

When you live in an apartment building, you have no control over who your neighbors might be. I didn't know this guy, but I'll never forget my glimpse of his apartment.

WHERE: My old building in the West 70s.

WHEN: Mid 1980s.

WHO: Building handyman; me.

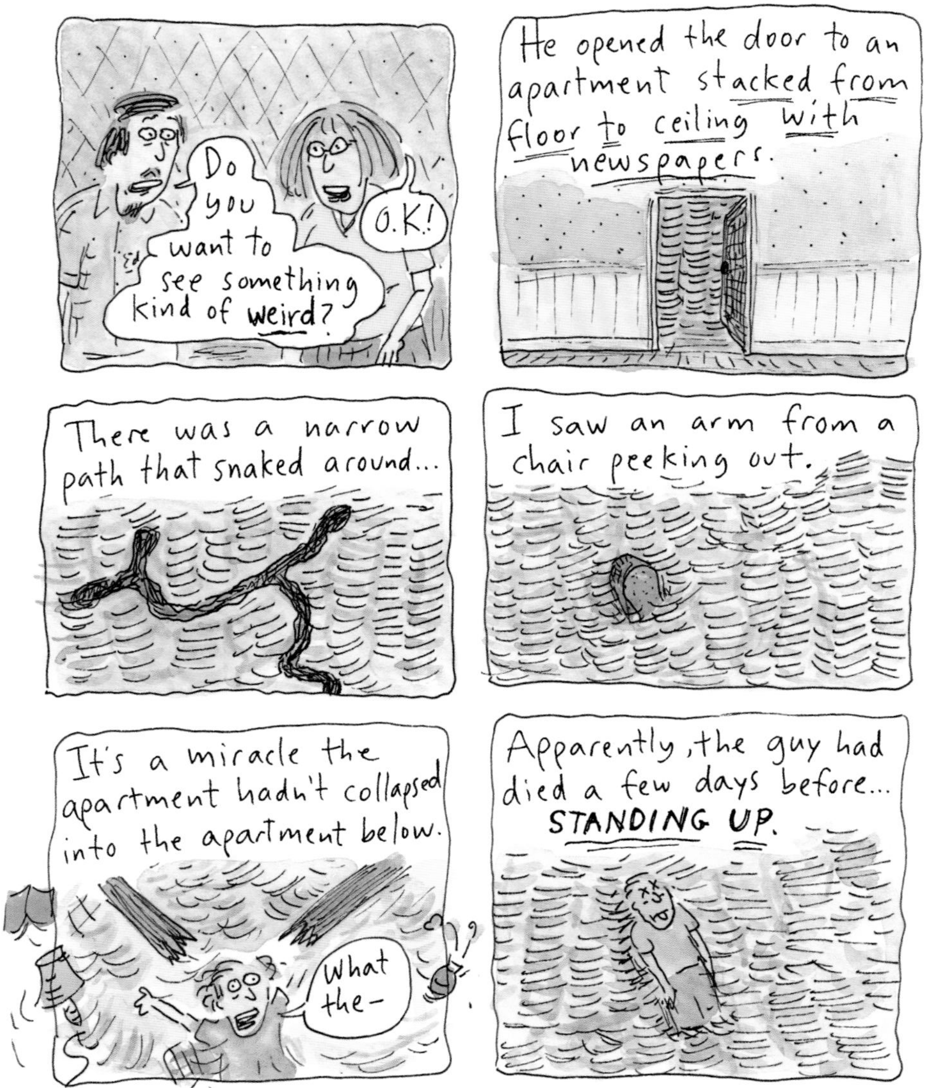

Do you want to see something kind of weird?
O.K.!
He opened the door to an apartment stacked from floor to ceiling with newspapers.
There was a narrow path that snaked around...
I saw an arm from a chair peeking out.
It's a miracle the apartment hadn't collapsed into the apartment below.
What the-
Apparently, the guy had died a few days before...
STANDING UP.

The greatest thing about living in an apartment house is that you have a SUPER. Theoretically, this means that you will never, ever have to deal with plumbing or electricity again.

Make friends with your super. By that, I don't mean take him out for lunch and tell him about all your personal problems. I mean treat him with great respect, and tip him as generously as your budget will allow, whenever he fixes something, and also at Christmastime.

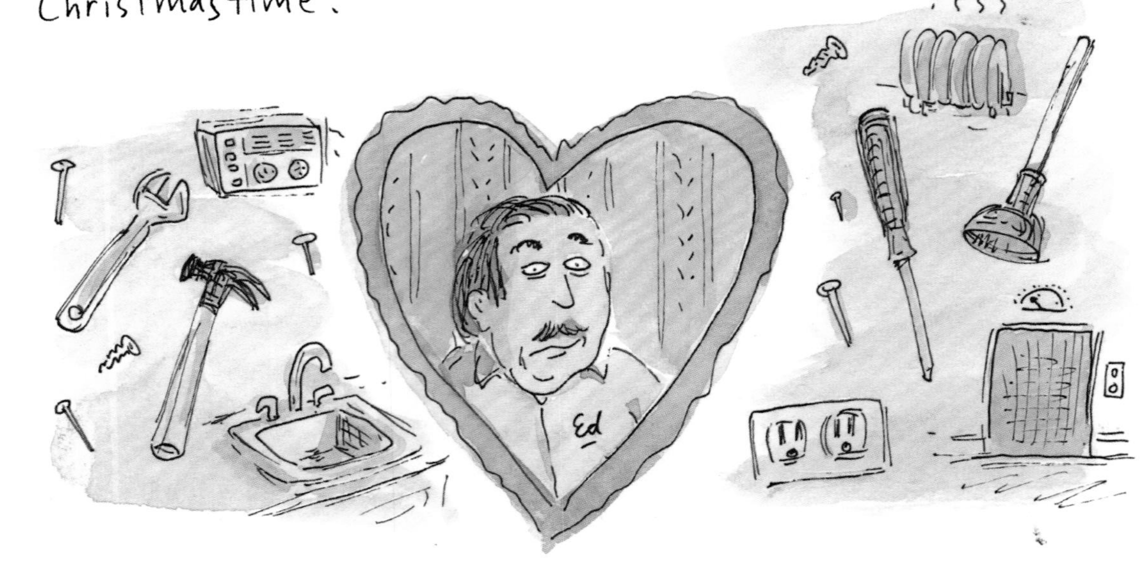
Ed

Finding an apartment in Manhattan if you're not a zillionaire is not easy. But it's also not impossible. If you do want to live here, you will probably have to recalibrate your idea of what is affordable, and also make a compromise or two.

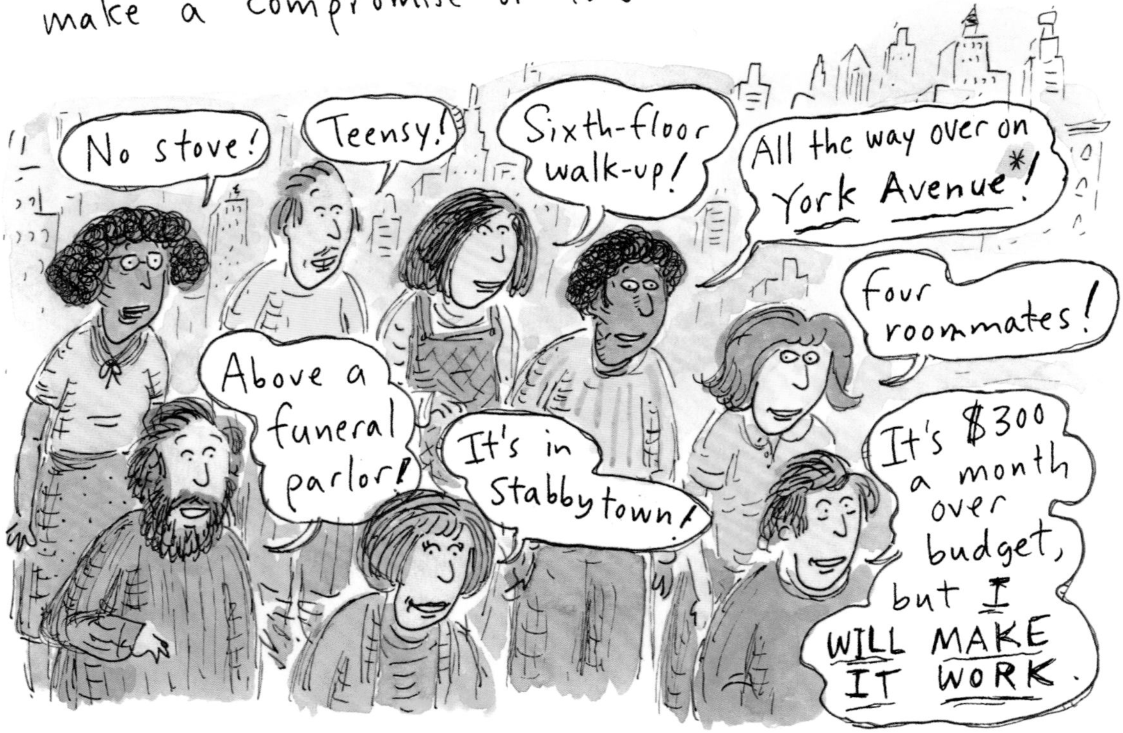
No stove!
Teensy!
Sixth-floor walk-up!
All the way over on York Avenue*!
four roommates!
Above a funeral parlor!
It's in Stabbytown!
It's $300 a month over budget, but I WILL MAKE IT WORK.

* York Avenue = extremely far eastern Manhattan. Practically in Europe.

WAYS TO FIND AN APARTMENT

- Online listings
- Newspaper
- Rental offices/broker (additional fee)
- Sign on lamp post
- Friend
- Nice doorman
- Obituaries
- Prayer
- Karma
- Hexes
- Magic secret apartment dance

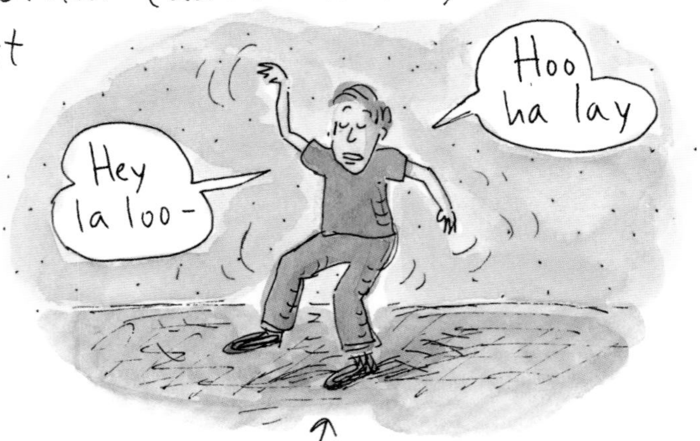

Hey la loo-
Hoo ha lay

- Shrine

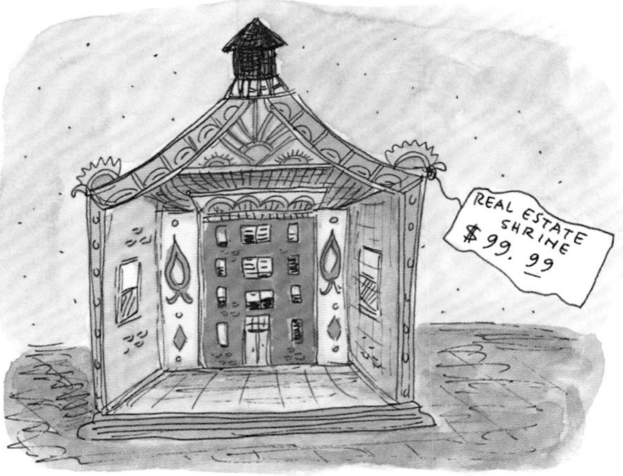

REAL ESTATE SHRINE $99.99

If you really want to live in Manhattan, don't listen to naysayers. It will happen.

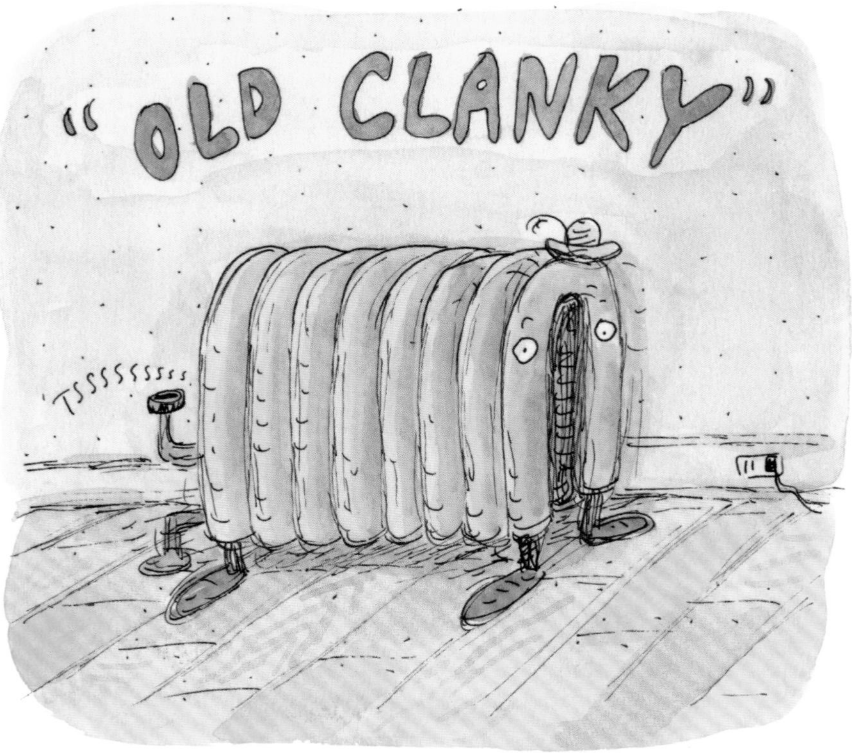
"OLD CLANKY"
TSSSSSSSSS

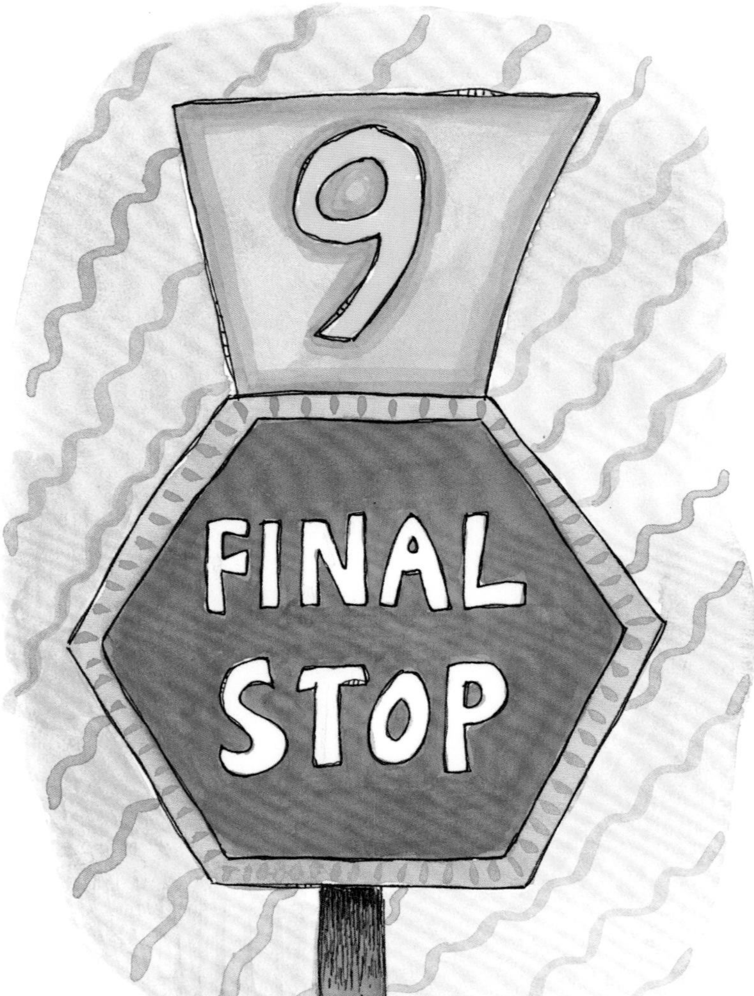
9
FINAL
STOP

In 1949, E.B. White wrote one of the best books ever written about New York City called Here is New York. In it, he wrote that there were essentially three New Yorks:

First, there was the New York of the person who was born here, who "takes the city for granted and accepts its size and its turbulence as natural and inevitable." Secondly, there is the New York of the daily commuter who arrives for work every morning and leaves every evening for home in the Suburbs. You will almost never see this New Yorker wandering around aimlessly or sitting on a park bench. The commuter gives New York its "tidal restlessness."

Last of all is the New York of the person who was "born somewhere else and came to New York in quest of something."

I didn't come to New York from Akron or Mumbai, but from deep Brooklyn, right across the East River. I moved to Manhattan to save myself from the life I had very clearly pictured as my destiny: living in a grim little apartment down the hall from my parents and commuting every day to Manhattan to a hateful, soul-deadening job. I saw myself on the train: middle-aged, wearing beige support hose and a dirty beige trench coat and some sort of horrible "office garb," clinging to a subway pole and wondering why I was ever born.

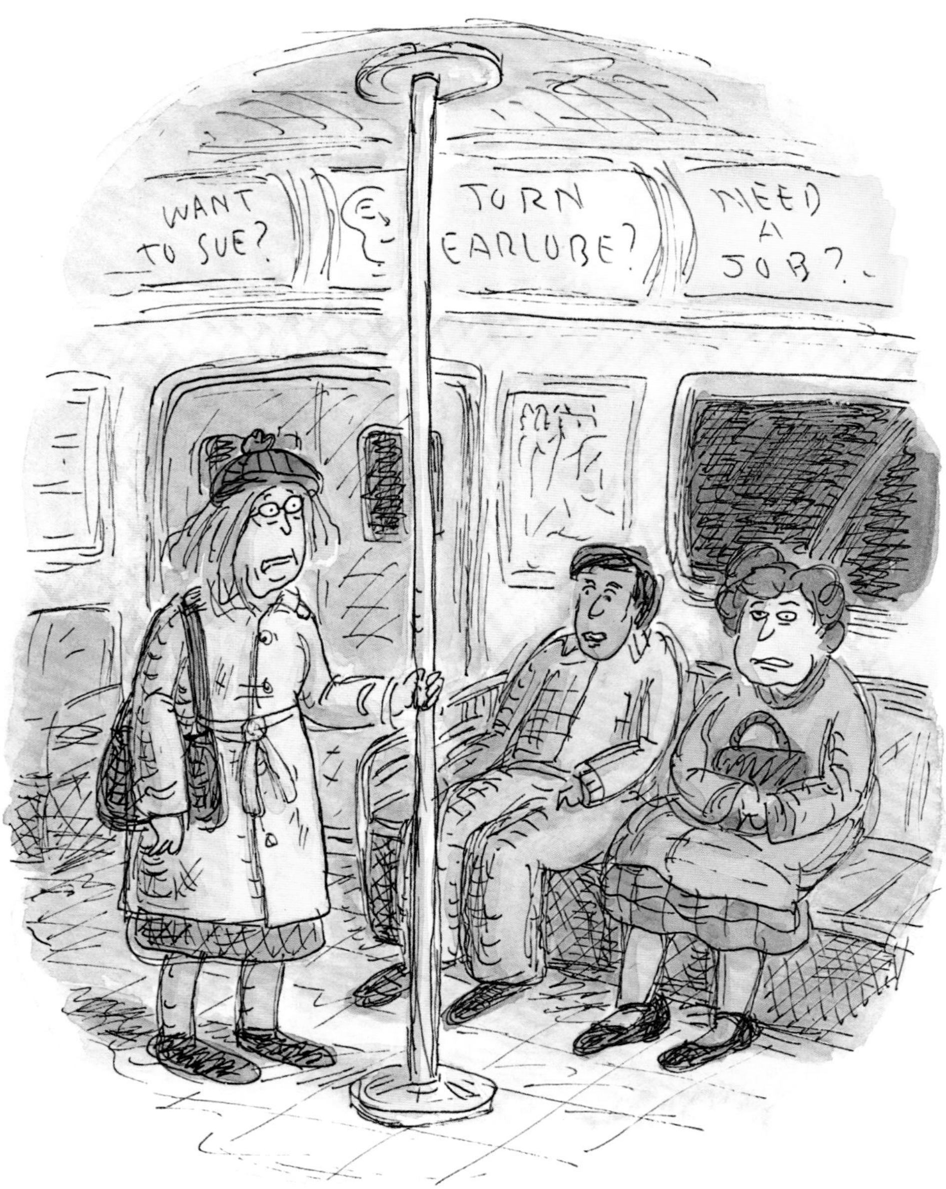
WANT TO SUE?
TORN EARLOBE?
NEED A JOB?

FUTURE ME

In some ways, I identify with all three groups. But it's with the last group, the "seekers from elsewhere" with whom I most identify.

I will always feel gratitude and astonishment that Manhattan allowed me to make my home there. It's still the only place I've been where I feel, in some strange way, that I fit in. Or maybe, that it's the place where I least feel that I _don't_ fit in.

New York is always changing. The New York of 2017 is different from the New York of 1983, and both of those versions are different from E.B. White's New York of 1949. I'm sure, in 2097, it will be something else again...

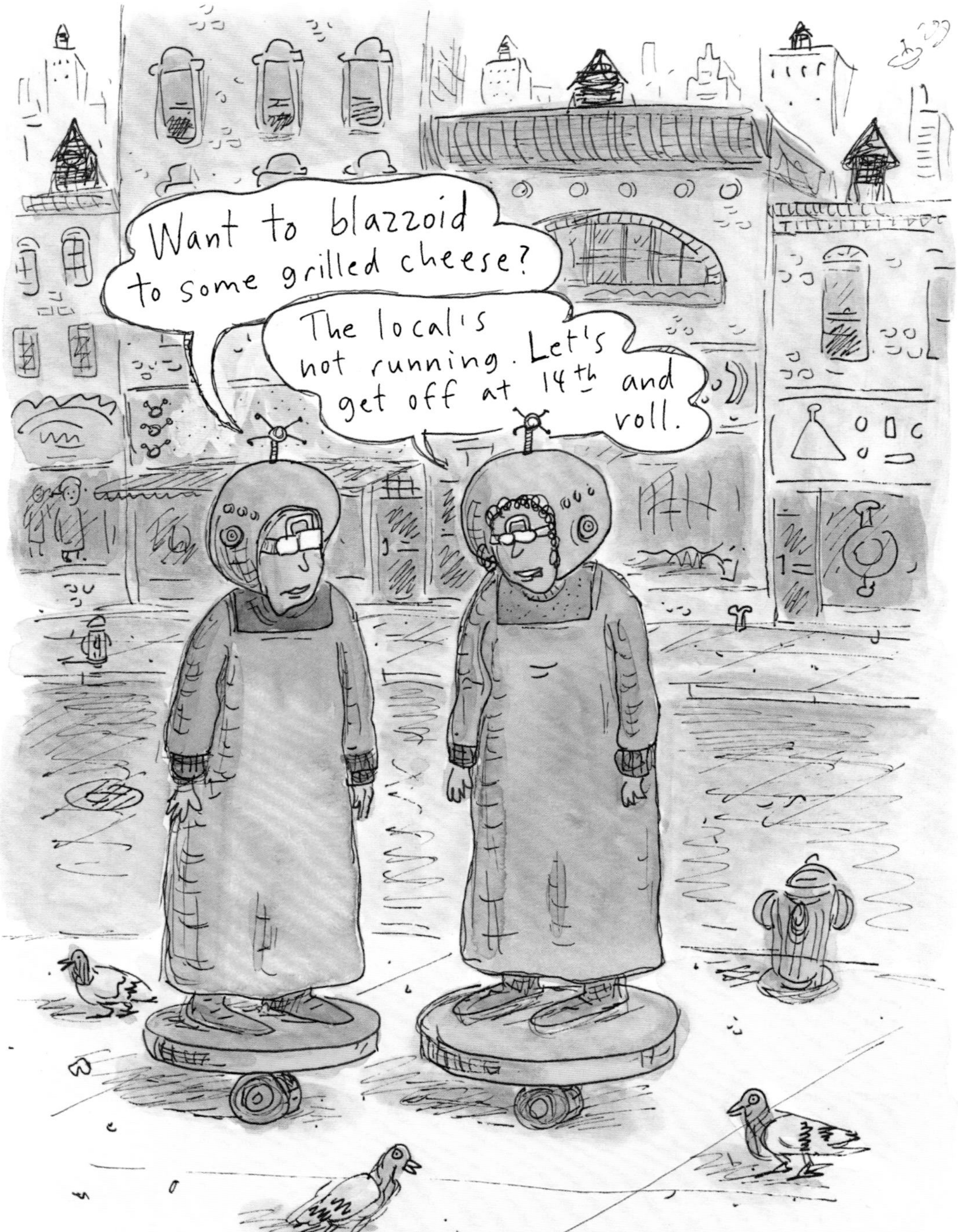
Want to blazzoid to some grilled cheese?
The local's not running. Let's get off at 14th and roll.

I try not to freak out every time a favorite restaurant or bookstore closes. I remind myself that life is change, and that life in New York is _definitely_ change, and that it's pointless to get overly sad because the place where you used to buy sketch pads is now a Jamba Juice.

I'm not nostalgic for the grittier, <u>Taxi Driver</u> incarnation of New York of the '70s and '80s. I don't miss the muggings, the shootings, the dog poop everywhere, not wanting to use the public restroom at Grand Central, the heroin, the graffiti (the "fuck you" kind, not the "cool" kind), AIDS, etc. I _do_ miss the cheaper rents.

New York is cleaner now, which is good, but also fancier. And I'm not such a big fan of fanciness.

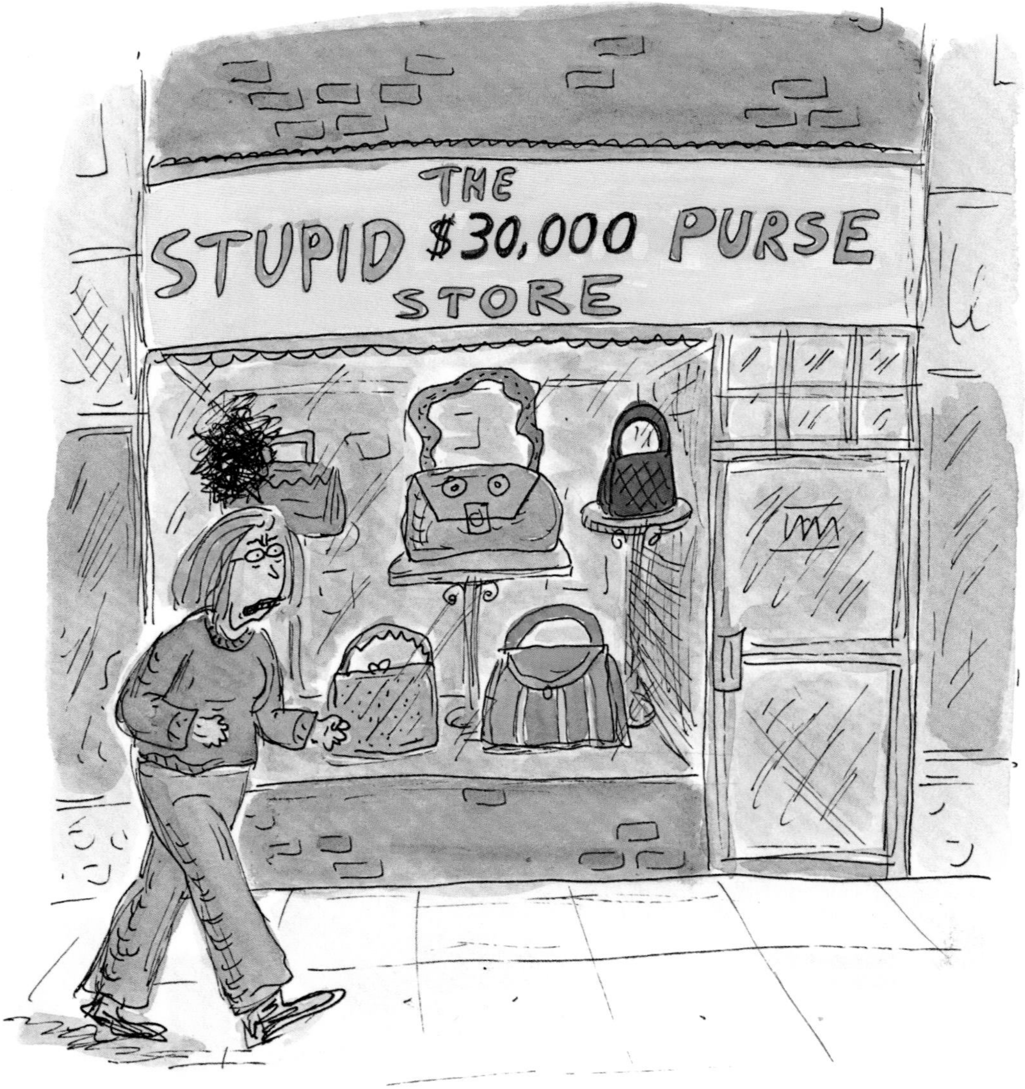
THE
STUPID $30,000 PURSE
STORE

The most profound change in New York
happened on September 11th, 2001, when —
out of NOWHERE — on a beautiful late-
summer day, two jet planes flew into the
twin towers of the World Trade Center.

In that instant, any illusion that we were
somehow immune to the horrors that happen
in so many other parts of the world vanished.

I thought it was the first time we —
New Yorkers — had ever lost our sense of
invulnerability, but I was mistaken.
To quote E.B. White again — from Here is
New York, written in the wake of World
War II, in 1949:

"The city, for the first time in its long history, is destructible. A single flight of planes... can quickly end this island fantasy, burn the towers, crumble the bridges, turn the underground passages into lethal chambers, cremate millions... All dwellers in cities must live with the stubborn fact of annihilation, {but} New York has a certain clear priority. In the mind of whatever perverted dreamer might loose the lightning, New York must hold a steady, irresistible charm."

But New York came back. This is the best place in the world, an experiment, a melting pot, a fight to the death, an opera, a musical comedy, a tragedy, none of the above, all of the above. We're a target for seekers and dreamers and also nuts. We live here anyway.

This book is a sort-of guide and also a thank-you letter and a love letter to my hometown and New Yorkers everywhere. You know who you are.

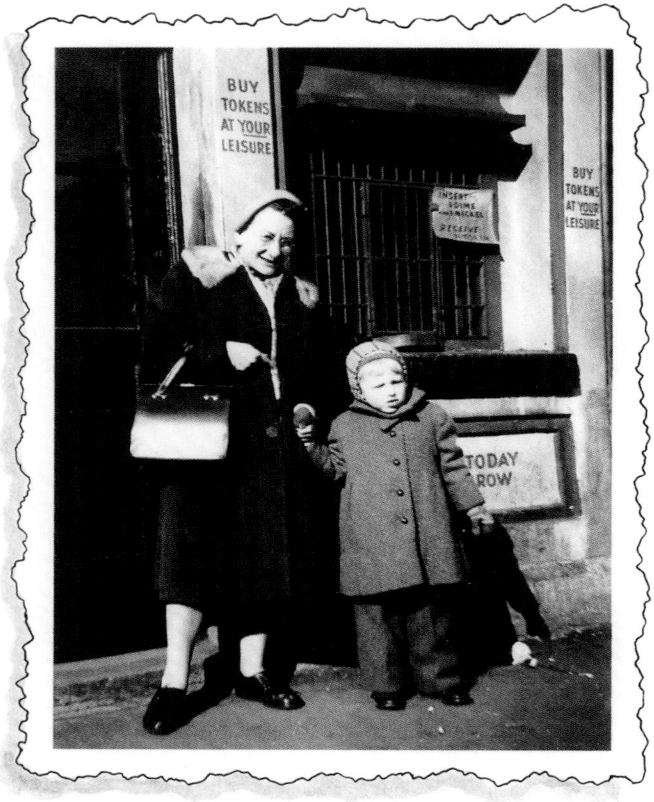
BUY TOKENS AT YOUR LEISURE
BUY TOKENS AT YOUR LEISURE
TODAY